A RELEVANT SALVATION

PREACHING FOR TODAY

A
RELEVANT
SALVATION

by

R. E. O. WHITE

Minister, Baptist Free Church
Boreham Wood, Herts.

Wm. B. Eerdmans Publishing Company
Grand Rapids, Michigan

First published 1963

PHOTOLITHOPRINTED BY CUSHING - MALLOY, INC.
ANN ARBOR, MICHIGAN, UNITED STATES OF AMERICA
1963

CONTENTS

Chapter   *Page*

THE MODERN MALAISE

1. Rootlessness: "We have no lasting city"   7
2. Aimlessness: "He . . . does not know where he goes"   14
3. Lostness: "Set up waymarks . . . make yourself guideposts"   21
4. Loneliness: "Jesus Himself drew near"   28
5. Faithlessness: "Because of their unbelief"   35
6. Lasciviousness: "The flesh with its passions"   42
7. Disintegration: "Unite my heart"   49
8. Humanism: "God is not man"   56
9. Transience: "Tomorrow we die"   63

A RELEVANT SALVATION

10. "The Opening of the Prison"—Religion as Liberation   70
11. "Like Treasure Hidden"—Religion as Discovery   76
12. Finding a Faith to Live By—Religion as Interpretation   82
13. Does Piety Pay?—Religion as Enrichment   89
14. "By These Things Men Live"—Religion as Accumulated Experience   96
15. "If God so Commands"—Religion as Moral Inspiration   102

16. Handling the Past—Religion as Absolution 109
17. Surprises Unlimited—Religion as Divine Intervention 116
18. "The Same . . . For Ever"—Religion as Invincible Truth 123
    Acknowledgements 130

I

ROOTLESSNESS

1

"I ENT GOT no roots . . ." protests Beatie despairingly in Arnold Wesker's timely play. "Roots! The things you come from, the things that feed you. The things that make you proud of yourself."

The playwright thus pinpoints a typical mid-century disorder: but twenty-five years earlier essentially the same problem was diagnosed in more solemn but not more accurate terms—

> Among the causes of modern man's maladjustment is "uprootedness". To be rooted is perhaps the most important and least recognized need of the human soul. It is one of the hardest to define. A human being has roots by virtue of his real, active and natural participation in the life of a community which preserves in living shape certain particular treasures of the past and certain particular expectations for the future. Every human being needs to have multiple roots. It is necessary for him to draw well nigh the whole of his moral, intellectual and spiritual life by way of the environment of which he forms a natural part.

That only spells out laboriously Wesker's crisper definition: roots are "the things you come from, the things that feed you".

Roots anchor, and nourish, and to some extent explain a man. They provide the invisible links by which an individual is held within his spiritual context, is nurtured by his social milieu, is "accounted for" by his time and origins, his education and his background. The pattern of every life is shaped by its assumptions,

7

its self-chosen point of view, its instinctive reactions, its accepted horizons of experience and of ambition: and all these are determined by the interaction of a man's nature with the environment into which his life is thrown. The innumerable invisible channels of that interaction are his "roots".

If the native soil of a man's life be itself but shifting sand, or if by his own restlessness or unhappy circumstance his roots be violently broken, then all too often he will drift, the starved and rootless offshoot of a shallow and unstable generation. The consequences of that kind of existence are familiar, and manifold.

Intellectually, rootlessness fosters an outlook inconstant and persuadable, easy prey to every glib demagogue and journalistic cliché, every fashionable prejudice and current dogma. Morally, it produces a chameleon character that takes colour from its immediate environment, falls in automatically with the standards of its "set", and counts it the deadliest of all the seven sins to be— just different. Emotionally, rootlessness suffers an acute awareness of not belonging—to any one, to any circle, to any where; a sense of inner isolation and sometimes of hostility, that rises to hysteria in the stateless refugee, the rejected delinquent, the repulsed alien, the racial outsider, but is present also in the chronic unhappiness of many intensely lonely people.

II

So described, rootlessness may seem a characteristically modern malady. Yet, like everything intrinsically human, it finds a scriptural expression.

The shrewd observation of a Hebrew poet sets in illuminating contrast the tree, deep-rooted by rivers of water, whose leaf does not wither and whose fruit does not fail, and the chaff, which the wind drives helter-skelter "away"—nowhere in particular, merely away, out of sight, endlessly on the move. So, permanence and productiveness alike depend on rootage. Jesus said the same when in a famous parable He likened certain people who made a fruitless religious profession to seed springing too quickly from shallow soil, and withering because "they have no root in themselves".

A related idea is found in the story of the barren fig-tree, for which the treatment prescribed was digging and manuring about the roots. Of essentially the same spiritual import is the trenchant warning of Jesus that branches severed from the Vine stock—cut off from their roots—can "do nothing".

Plainly this business of root-cultivation is an abiding human concern. Psychiatry may fairly be said to be a highly developed skill in root-investigation and root-pruning—the search among the subterranean forces of personality for those hidden motivations, compulsions and fears which so mysteriously bear sour fruit in conscious life. Education, in one of its major functions, is the rooting of a new generation in the culture and wisdom of the past, that it may be nourished thereby and develop therefrom, whether by evolution or revolt. Religion too has to do with the root-system of the individual soul, the permanent soil and background from which thought and aspiration and feeling spring and by which they are sustained. That is why the greatest immediate reward of a religious life is the capacity to live from a great depth of being.

III

But modern conditions aggravate this abiding human concern into an intimate and acute problem for many people. One practical difficulty is, to stay long enough in one place to achieve any depth of friendship, of social integration, even of simple appreciation of one's neighbours and the life going on around one.

Ours is a mobile society. "A century ago," says F. W. Boreham in a nostalgic lament over the modern fondness for moving house, "A century ago the removal of an English family from one village to another was regarded as a social tragedy through all the countryside. A man worked for his master because his father had worked for his master's father, and his grandfather for his master's grandfather, and it never occurred to him that some social cataclysm might prevent his grandchildren from working for his master's grandchildren. All this has changed."

And how! We are all nomads now: and if the motel and the auto-caravan have replaced the camel-trains and covered wagons, the psychological and spiritual consequences of a life without roots have not lessened.

Yet even amidst this social restlessness, this endless peripatetic migration that equates "hometown" with "stagnation" and measures progress by the speed with which we can arrive at the next place we intend to leave, a sensibly tended religious background to life is an immense practical advantage. For in each new encampment, some circle of Christian friends and fellow-worshippers can be discovered, given the patience and a little trouble, and immediate spiritual transplantation is possible for oneself, one's family, and—not least important—for one's children.

A familiar soil of common beliefs, an atmosphere of Christian fellowship and aspiration, the shade of congenial moral and social standards cast by a revered tradition as to what is Christian, an accustomed climate of prayer and worship, all await the incoming stranger who will make an effort to send down his spiritual roots in a new plot but to the same nourishing springs that flow from God through Christ. The perambulating Christian, even in our disrupted Western society, even across the globe in almost-forgotten corners of dark continents, is assured of half-made friendships ready to be completed as he seeks out fellow-believers, and finds in the Name of Jesus an already charged magnetic contact that sparks immediately into sincere interest, welcome, and comradeship.

IV

But the problem of spiritual rootage is more than a by-product of twentieth-century mobility. We must not allow the metaphor to run away with us, and suppose that merely standing still is enough to nourish the soul. We cannot evade the truth that "here we have no lasting city". The opening lines of Homer's *Odyssey* echo the earliest pages of the Old Testament in likening human life to a journey and man to a pilgrim, unavoidably moved on by nature, time, events and experience combined—and even more by his own ambition, discontent, and aspiration. The only adequate roots a moving spirit can retain are roots among eternal things, realities that remain amid all time's changes and grow and move with man's development and understanding. The background of every pilgrimage is the eternal desert, the over-arching sky, the fixed horizon, the steadfast religious tradition, the sacred ideal and the unalterable goal, and the avowed purpose that is not to be deflected by threats or weather, discomfort or danger.

In fact, it is always the things that do not move or change that give to all human progress its meaning, its measurement, its significance and value.

In this far more compelling sense of the eternal background to a changing time, modern man feels a desperate need of roots: by every new discovery of prehistory and of astronomy he is made poignantly aware that in some sense he does not "belong" on this wandering star of a world. A famous Cambridge astronomer of our own time has remarked, while discussing the odd contrast between the material that constitutes the sun and that which is abundant on the earth and nearby planets: "The earth is the freak. You must understand that, cosmically speaking, the room you are now sitting in is made of the wrong stuff. You yourself are odd. You are a rarity, a cosmic collector's piece."

Not entirely a cosy thought! We, and our earth-home, "do not belong" where we find ourselves; we are all aliens. Yet we desperately need somewhere to feel at home, some trend of things with which to feel at one, some final understanding in which to be at rest.

And the need is met. What Sir James Jeans said about the modern conception of the cosmos, that "the immensity of the universe becomes a matter of satisfaction rather than awe; we are citizens of no mean city", another has said about God, that

> . . . greatness which is infinite makes room
>   For all things in its lap to lie;
> We should be crushed by a magnificence
>   Short of Infinity.
> But what is infinite must be a home,
>   A shelter, for the meanest life . . .

Such shelter, anchorage, dwelling-place, in all generations, is the eternal God, into whose steadfast love all man's roots go down.

V

This is precisely the theme of the ninetieth Psalm. With seven quick strokes the poet depicts man's life as a journey through a wilderness, brief, insecure, impermanent. All about him is the "dust" to which God so soon bids man return. Though the grass springs fresh and swift in the heavy morning dew, it fades and is bleached before evening comes, even as man's glory dies. A passing bird suggests how swiftly and silently man himself flies away; the rushing torrent of the new-filled *wadi* recalls the stream of time that bears away the generations. A man's story is soon told, like an eastern tale beside the evening fire: follows a short, dream-filled sleep beneath the stars, or perhaps the sentry's vigil before he too is relieved from duty to seek his rest. "Life passeth soon."

But this is not the whole story. The pilgrim spirit of mankind has its home—the background out of which man came, the goal towards which he tends. Without this, the journeying lacks beginning and meaning and end, becomes a dreary wandering in a maze, a lost child's endless to and fro in unknown streets. So, over against the swirling dust, the rushing stream, the short sleep, the shrivelled grass, the brief vigil, the passing bird, the long sweep of history "in all generations", are set deliberately the emblems of permanence: the immovable mountains, the solid, unchanging face of the earth persisting through the passing seasons, the measureless visible backdrop of sun, moon and stars, timelessly the same, and the eternal, invisible God, there before them all, and still there when they are gone.

Man moves, and grows, and journeys, and passes away. Yet he has roots among eternal things: a clear and satisfying intellectual anchorage in a simple, unshifting faith in the eternal God; a strong and satisfying moral shelter in a reverent, unaccommodating code; a deep and satisfying emotional resource in the comfort of divine love. In God we live *and move* and have our being, and the soul of man homes upon God. For "all our springs are in Thee".

2

AIMLESSNESS

I

HUMANITY'S most obvious missing component is a built-in direction-finder, some psychological equivalent of the automatic pilot that mechanically and unerringly finds its own way home. Even that crown and consummation of human ingenuity, the space capsule, if it misses its planned trajectory, can only be destroyed: from which man himself might learn that his incapacity to see ahead, combined with his tendency to go wrong, is his direst peril. Walking in darkness he does not know where he goes, but he is fairly sure to arrive where he did not wish to get!

Walter Lippmann, America's most observant commentator, surprised many friends of the United States by declaring: "We talk about ourselves these days as if we were a completed society, one which . . . has no further great business to transact. The question is whether this country can recover what for the time being it does not have—a sense of great purpose. That is the crucial point." Crucial indeed, but if the world's most go-ahead nation does not know where it is going, who does?

Almost contemporaneous with Lippmann's remark came a report on youthful anti-social behaviour in one of Britain's new towns, in which the prevailing explanation offered by the young themselves reiterated the phrase "There's nothing to do—the place is pretty dead." That, at an age when strength should overflow, ambition blaze, dreams beckon commandingly, and time be all too short for all youth wants to do! A pompous, but not

14

undiscerning, comment on the popularity of Rock 'n' Roll described it as an orgy of irrational emotionalism, socially useful as a mopper-up of undirected energies otherwise liable to explode.

"There's nothing to do": a Yorkshire novelist attending the missionary commissioning of a school friend, though herself standing outside the religious faith and fervour of the occasion, felt deeply its inspiration and excitement but returned home to confide to her diary the pathetic cry which sounds too often in the heart of our generation—"Oh, if only there were something worth dedicating oneself to, utterly and for ever!"

It is the cry of a soul with capacities, and ardour, and readiness to be challenged, but profoundly bored with a life that has neither purpose nor meaning nor aim. Nor is that mood confined to the detached, sensitive observer of life. Aldous Huxley, out of an unrivalled breadth of experience, describes how modern men "move through life hollow with pointlessness, trying to fill the void within them by external stimuli—newspaper reading, day-dreaming at the films, radio music and chattering, playing, or above all the watching, of games, 'good times' of every sort. Meantime any doctrine that offers to restore point and purpose to life is eagerly welcomed." And all this elaboration of the trivial, together with the constant tendency towards "subhuman emotion and animality—hence the craving for narcotics and stimulants, and the never-failing attraction of the crowd", Huxley links directly to "our conviction that the world is meaningless".

This seems but a modern, prosy version of an ancient poetic answer to the undying question "What is your life?"—"It is but a vapour", insubstantial, evanescent, unsatisfying, valueless, aimless. We are, after all, the first generation in history to make an industry out of entertaining ourselves, and to reward with princely incomes and unprecedented glory those who help us to pass the tedious time.

Electronic miracles of incredible ingenuity sustain a wholly fictitious world of passionate romance, hair-breadth escapes, space espionage and wits-against-the-law, to provide a daily ration of excitement for minds dulled and spirits bored by repetitive work, trivial interests, and vacant goals. An entirely manufactured risk, spiced with greed, gives gambling its fascination, and countless thousands seek in the pretended contests of professional sport the zest and purpose and driving ambition which real life in the twentieth century so rarely achieves.

The feeling of futility is not new: Hobbes long ago coined the effective phrase to describe life without religious perspectives: "ignorant, poor, nasty, brutish, and short". Shakespeare's version,

> it is a tale
> Told by an idiot, full of sound and fury
> Signifying nothing.

is no less terrible when shorn of its poetry. But the feeling is sharply intensified in our generation by the repeated and widespread frustration of high hopes that our century has known. What is new, moreover, is the solemn and reasoned conviction that life itself is purposeless, and man's whole existence insignificant—and this after an era of "inevitable progress" when science, education and technology were to make of human life an endless paradise.

Several concurrent influences contribute to this mood. Modern astronomy has pushed back the walls of the universe until its magnitude baffles imagination: a universe too big to measure, expanding at a speed too fast to calculate, leaves Mother Earth a mere speck of star-dust upon which man in his countless millions, with all his hopes and loves and dreams and loyalties and faith, is infinitesimally small and cosmically negligible. Fred Hoyle's remark, that "perhaps the most majestic feature of our whole existence is that while our intelligences are powerful enough to penetrate deeply into the evolution of this quite incredible universe, we still have not the smallest clue to our own fate" is a frank confession that science has lost its sense of direction.

The literary fashion which debunks the great causes that once fired men's souls for freedom, equality, justice, knowledge, and peace, and which "exposes" the great men who once were heroes, has helped powerfully to rob life of noble purpose. Nor can one measure the effect upon a whole generation's faith and social drive of the continual emphasis upon a psychological determinism which leaves man helpless to control his future, all human prospects being pre-ordained by environmental, racial, hereditary, social, subconscious and material forces which man can diagnose but not direct.

Sociologically, the bloc vote, the political machine, the impersonal pressure group, have had the same effect of submerging individual initiative, reinforced by popular acceptance of the sovereignty of economic considerations, market "trends", and monetary and commercial "laws", which must take precedence over private conscience, taste, and aspiration. So, for very many, life is reduced to a meaningless routine of shallow interests and insignificant obligations: if man strives at all, it is too often towards goals he no longer deeply believes in, amid a chorus of derisive voices, and carrying in his nervous hands all-powerful toys he does not know how to use, and dare not throw away.

In such a context, individual hearts have somehow to live out their own destinies, snatching such happiness as they may, endeavouring to give some meaning to their days, defending themselves as best they can against adversity, hardship, illness, and the fear of death, and hoping against hope that it all gets somewhere in the end.

II

"He who walks in the darkness does not know where he goes." Jesus well knew the dangers, and the despair, of that settled futility that finds nothing worth the doing. He saw how a

2

vacuous, pointless existence left the soul of man, like an empty house, prey to invasion by devils of all kinds, mischief, despondency, bitterness, despair, until some dominating, life-fulfilling purpose claimed possession. He knew how many stand idle in the marketplace of life, spiritually unemployed, complaining weakly that "no man has hired us". He was aware too how often the rich talent lies buried beneath some soil of self-pity, injured self-importance, slothfulness, or fear of responsibility—making life profitless by sheer want of aim and true ambition. How very often Jesus condemned the things left undone, the barrenness of privileged lives, the good unthought of, or unpursued, the needy neglected, all because men see no purpose demanding dedication, and feel no challenging aim that draws them out of selfishness to serve a cause greater than themselves.

Christ lived under the constant compulsion of great purposes: and hard though it is to make the leap from our bewildered generation, where men without a creed grope blindly along unmapped roads towards unforeseeable destinations, back to the sublime simplicities of Galilee, yet if we make the effort and in imagination walk with Jesus beside the inland sea, we shall discover at least three things relevant to this modern need.

We shall find Him stopping oftentimes to talk with individuals, pausing in a crowd to speak comfortingly to one shrinking woman, going—literally—out of His way to heal a child, inviting Himself to dine with an outcast "sinner". We shall hear Him talk in terms of deliberate exaggeration about the hairs of each head being numbered, about the value of one soul being beyond all creatures, beyond all sacred institutions, beyond the value of all the world.

We shall see Him constantly setting each human life against the background of eternity, extending to an infinite perspective each individual's struggle and worth and hope. We shall find Him living and teaching in calm assurance of a divine love that is outpoured upon every child of God. And He never once spoke of humanity: always of you, and you, and you. Vast though the universe may be, it is no vaster than His Father's heart—and there the individual is never lost.

We shall find Jesus, secondly, speaking much of a divine purpose into which each individual life may be fitted, to grow indefinitely in significance and personal value by its place within the total scheme. Jesus called men from their nets and desks and homes to follow Him upon an endless quest for a better world; He welded those who responded into a team of dedicated men, a community in which none loses freedom or importance but in which each finds an infinitely richer aim in life than he could discover elsewhere. "Others have laboured," Jesus said, "and you have entered into their labour."

All this He could do, for and with very ordinary folk of the villages and towns of a small provincial district, because for His mind, behind all history lies God's will, behind all human society stands God's kingdom, awaiting perfect manifestation and final fulfilment. Even man's folly and sin may be reshaped to ultimate good as men surrender to that will, and serve the cause of that divine ideal. Nor is this mere optimism masquerading as religious faith. All scientific inquiry assumes the world has order, reason, discoverable pattern, at the heart of it. Says Professor E. de C. Andrade, quoting Newton's confession of faith in a Supreme Being, Lord over all, "lesser men than Newton, confronted with harder questions, need not be ashamed to fall back upon divine purpose for an answer."

Certainly not when he does so in the company of Jesus. Wide and sweeping as the onward movement of the universe may be, it is not more all-embracing than His Father's purpose of good; and within that purpose every man becomes significant, his life-work adding its unique contribution to the kingdom's ultimate success, and nothing being lost.

So man need not walk in darkness, not knowing where he goes. We find in Jesus, thirdly, the light of the world—a beacon, a beckoning gleam, a torchlight blazing the trail to Christlike living in a Christlike world. To reject His leadership is to accept futility. But to follow Him is to be ever at the start of great adventure, ever totally engaged to endless, world-wide enterprise, ever headed homewards toward's life's goal, in God.

> From Thee, great God, we spring, to Thee we tend,
> Path, motive, guide, original, and end.

3

LOSTNESS

I

THE PROPHET'S exhortation is strictly a call to hope. The
tribes of northern Israel are passing into cruel captivity, but
Jeremiah commands that they "keep their voice from weeping
and their eyes from tears, for they shall come back from the land
of the enemy. There is hope for your future . . . and your children
shall come back to their own country." And that they might
find their way home, "Set up waymarks . . . make yourself
guideposts." For the desert was perilous to strangers if the stone
pillars that marked the tracks were removed, or buried. The
importance of road-signs to road-safety is evidently no modern
discovery!

Nevertheless, the removal of landmarks and the destruction
of guideposts has been a characteristic of the twentieth century.
In the last three generations, signposts and boundaries and moral
road-warnings of all kinds have been obscured or destroyed with
cheerful zeal—sometimes rebelliously, sometimes irresponsibly,
often in the name of a specious freedom that disguises confusion,
excuses indiscipline, and hides from man himself how completely
he—unaided—will miss his way.

A host of influences contribute to this dangerous delight in
getting lost. With the rise of democracy came the idea that all
opinions are equally valid, and truth can be known by its
popularity: authority is "out"! With increased communications
has come the impact of non-Christian cultures, with very
different values and behaviour-codes, upon the young minds of

the West already unsettled by harsh experience. A widening educational gulf between old and young has helped much to destroy parental authority and undermine home restraints. The moral shattering of two world wars, in which the most serious casualties were truth, justice, kindness, compassion, and faith, left behind an intense confusion of conscience and tradition.

The theory of evolution challenged long accepted principles of human dignity and conduct: behaviourist accounts of thought and conscience destroyed confidence in both truth and goodness: the attack of science upon biblical doctrine, of liberalism and anti-clericalism upon the Church, of the spirit of free and factual inquiry upon all dogma, of radicalism upon every kind of autocracy—including that of moral and intellectual excellence— —all combined to produce an attitude of relativism in philosophy, of rebelliousness and experimentation in conduct, of distrust of all authority and law, of contempt for all conventions, until no absolute truth remains, and "nothing's good or bad but thinking makes it so".

In such a world-view, the ancient landmarks that ensured man's safety have gone, the guideposts are buried beneath the barren sand of denials and scepticism, and the new generation flounders, undirected and unled, amid a babble of contradictory voices, in a wilderness of uncharted but enticing paths. That is being lost: and none are so lost as they who do not know it.

> The World has forgotten its Home
> And the things that belong to its Peace.
> If our compass fail
> Our footsteps stagger and reel
> And all our marchings nothing avail
> But to bring us back on ourselves in circles,
> In dizzying, nightmare, maniac rings
> From whence is no release . . .
>
> The World is lost, and is looking for the Way.

So complains a poet of our time, and in such an unmapped world
the puzzled individual must find his way—and at the first attempt:
he has no second chance.

Those born into such an age of mists and quicksands, of denials,
contradictions and confusions, deserve utmost sympathy. Many
will cry with the young man in the gospels "What shall I do to
inherit eternal life?" but find no one to look on them with love
and answer with insight and divine authority. Many will plead
with the psalmist "How can a young man keep his way pure?"
and find no answering word of God to which he may take heed.

In such a time the heart is thrown back upon its own spiritual
insights and the inward authority of truth shining by its own
light. So Jesus appealed to the common judgement of earnest
men: "Why do you not judge for yourselves what is right?" No
man need be left entirely forlorn; truth *is* self-luminous, and "the
spirit of man is the candle of the Lord"—lighted, as Ben Which-
cote said, by God, and lighting us to God. It may be but a
second-best means of finding one's direction, but certain waymarks remain clear in the most confused wilderness, to those who
look within.

II

For example, he is not wholly lost who steadfastly remembers
that truth itself is sacred, and conquers in the end. When a man
thinks that any opinion he chooses to form, to which prejudice,
or self-interest, or ignorance, or self-will, has led him, is as good
as any other man's, and must be true because he holds it strongly,
then intellectually he is lost indeed. Until he recognizes that facts
are stubborn, and no less facts for being unpalatable; that truth
endures, and no less certainly for being denied; and that he had
better accept the universe, for he cannot alter it, and closing his
eyes only makes him blind—until, that is to say, he begins to look
for truth and not merely for confirmation of his own opinion,
he is not likely to find his way.

The arrogance of unbelief is no less a hindrance to clear

thinking than is the dogmatism of faith. It is true that the unshakeable conviction of the Christian concerning the things he surely believes is irritating and often repellent to those who do not share it. The Christian *knows* that God is, and is the rewarder of them who diligently seek Him, for he has found it so. He knows that Christ holds the key to all ultimate questions about man's origin, duty, and destiny, for he has found light to walk by and serenity of mind in following Him. He knows, too, that truth endures, and whatever reformulation of statement may be made necessary by new insights, the essential faith of countless generations of the world's saintliest men and women cannot be basically wrong.

Sometimes the Christian would do well to distinguish the certainties that rest on his personal experience of God—about which he can entertain no doubts—from the opinions which rest upon the particular environment in which his religious life developed—about which he would do well to be humble and open-minded. But the counsel is no less salutary for the inquirer, bemused by the sceptical denials of ancient affirmations. The man to whom truth is sacred will not lightly brush aside the massive testimony of those who have found in religious faith guideposts and clues as yet beyond his own experience. Nor will he suppose that denial and challenge form any final resting-place for intelligent minds. As the most hygienic man cannot actually live upon disinfectants, so the most clever and logical cannot find his way merely by the things he refuses to believe—he must find better.

And when unbelief has left him pathless and lost, he will be ready to challenge his own assumptions, to doubt his own doubts, to question the relevance of his own questions, and follow a little more humbly wherever honesty shall lead—lest he never find the way.

For all truth is God's: but only the free mind sees it, only the honest mind reverences it, only the courageous mind holds it firmly and follows it fearlessly. But given these qualities of earnestness, the truth will disclose itself; "he that seeketh findeth", and God is very willing to be found.

III

A man is not wholly lost, either, if he steadfastly values goodness beyond all else, counts moral cowardice the supreme disgrace, and moral failure the only final tragedy. When a man knows he must do right though the heavens fall; when he deeply believes that "if a thing is right it should be done, and if it should it can"; when he holds against all temptation and sophistry that personal integrity is more important than happiness, success, or ease; and when he accepts that defeat is never disgraceful until it breeds despair—then he is not far from the kingdom of heaven.

Such a man will soon discover among his own hard-won convictions that the universe is on the side of right, that the frame of things is moral, that harvest unerringly follows the pattern of the seedtime. And so believing he will find a hundred complex situations simplified and a confused way straighten itself out. For to the honest heart honestly seeking what is good, daylight surely breaks.

Love of truth and reverence for goodness are immeasurably strengthened if a man in danger of losing his way will cleave to the principle that in all circumstances his first and last obligation is to act in love. Whether he thinks of love, with Albert Schweitzer, as reverence for life, and so resolves ever to hold all living creatures as in every way superior in a universe of things; or whether he thinks of love, with Harry Fosdick, as just undiscourageable, unmeasured, unconfined goodwill; or whether he thinks of love quite simply as personal friendship indefinitely extended, will not be of first importance. All definitions aside, he will know what it means in practice to love his neighbour, and he will soon realize that such love "fulfils the whole law": from it all other duties and virtues derive their meaning and their obligation.

A man may reach that moral insight without any profound religious faith, and scarcely aware that he is borrowing it from Christ. It is doubtful if he will persevere in his resolve unless he comes somehow to believe that such an attitude is in the last resort in line with the current of life, and so comes within sight of the truth that God is love. But meanwhile he will have found, in the supremacy of love, a waymark and a guidepost that will direct his feet safely though the horizon and the goal be shrouded still in mist.

IV

A man in earnest about finding his way will soon discover that the attainment of truth, goodness, and love depends less upon environment, culture and social context than upon one's inner resources of insight, sympathy, and strength. Psychology will explain to him, what practical experience of moral endeavour will make abundantly plain, the supreme importance of that half-hidden mental hinterland from which our conscious life is drawn and fed. The whole meaning of faith and prayer and worship will be illuminated as he realizes that character is fashioned and nourished in the secret places of mind and heart, and that the only resources available for intellectual integrity and moral achievement lie in that spiritual world where religious aspiration and devotion make their discoveries.

By which time, his feet will be upon the homeward road, his confusions thinning out, and he will find that he walks no longer alone.

For the second-best means of finding one's direction is not good enough: life is too precious, the problems are too many, the cost of failure is too high. Safer by far the experience of the writer of the best-loved poem in the world—

> The Lord is my Guide.
> He leads me by true paths,
> as He himself is true.

My road may run through some dark ravine,
But I fear no harm;
For Thou art beside me—
Thy club to protect,
Thy staff to lean upon,
Provide my strength.

A guide is better than a map, a hero more satisfying, for heart and head, than many maxims; and it is the function of the hero, as Carlyle reminded us, to enlighten and enhearten, to kindle and constrain, to show what is possible and lure us to try. What better, indeed what *other* hero, for the heart that has lost its way, than He who declared "I am the way . . . Follow Me"?

I am glad to think
I am not bound to make the world go right;
But only to discover and to do,
With cheerful heart, the work which God appoints.
I will trust in Him,
That He can hold His own; and I will take
His will, above the work He sendeth me,
To be my chiefest good.

And He shall be my Guide, even unto death.

4

LONELINESS

I

IT IS curious that our age, which inherited so many and various problems, should contrive to invent a new one of its own; even more curious that, being the age of improved communications, and travel, and socialization, and collective experiments, and democracy, and community-centres and Social Man, its new and peculiar problem should be—loneliness.

Of course the weakening of family life, resulting both from increasing sexual freedom and from the speed of change that divides the generations, separates many individuals from the natural context of kinsfolk and blood-relationship in which, in former generations, each life was formerly spent. The world-ramifications of great business organizations and vast industries help to break up and scatter each family unit; and sometimes a close-knit rural community is invaded by industry demanding an elastic labour-force, until village and hometown explode into "conurbations" than which no place on earth in all history is more devastatingly lonely.

The drift of the younger generation to towns and cities for entertainment, opportunity, education, culture, or mere anonymity, throws many lives out of community and provides no substitute. Increasing longevity and decreasing families mean an ageing population in many areas, and such are the natural nostalgia and reserve of advancing years that age itself too often spells loneliness. Impoverished family loyalties and smaller dwellinghouses share some of the blame for that bitterness.

Bereavement, bachelorhood, only-child-hood, or a physical handicap that limits life to one room, bring the same sharp problem of isolation. Sometimes, the decay of religious fellowship, and of all the rich friendships it once fed, leaves unabsorbed many who formerly would have been socially integrated, unconsciously and automatically, by the practice of piety. Secularized suburbia has very little social cohesiveness, except the very artificial and often shallow "community-fostering" which scarcely does more than emphasize the need. The fierce competitiveness of a get-rich-quick-at-all-costs philosophy leaves little time or inclination for the cultivation of friendships that may contribute nothing to advancement.

In addition, of course, a great deal of loneliness is the result of desertion, or neglect, of recoil from family obligations, rebellion from family standards, of rejection, and of shame. With so many contributory causes, it is not surprising that the isolation of individuals from their fellows is a close burden and a heartache to so many modern people. If the mid-nineteenth century could complain, poetically and impersonally,

> Yes, in the sea of life enisled,
>   With echoing straits between us thrown,
> Dotting the shoreless, watery wild,
>   We mortal millions live alone

—in the mid-twentieth century the only adequate analogies would be drawn from the swirling star-dust amid the receding galaxies in the lonely immensities of space!

II

At the same time, pastoral experience suggests that loneliness has sometimes the inevitability of a vicious circle. Isolation can breed a resentful independence; friendlessness become unfriendliness, and what unfortunate circumstances imposed may become the occasion for bitter hostility, sometimes against those who deserve little reproach.

To be left alone demands, like any other affliction or misfortune, intelligent and resolute handling, an organizing of the lonely life that shall take full account of its opportunities and its dangers, a self-knowledge that shall frankly anticipate the effects of loneliness upon character, and a positive and continuous effort to make new friends—and not simply wait to be visited and consoled.

In the last analysis, affliction and bereavement aside,

> He only is alone
> Who lives not for another. Come what will,
> The generous man has his companion still.

For of course isolation from the pressure of social obligations is not all loss, or problem. To be alone is sometimes uniquely enriching: and though solitude is not by any means the same thing as loneliness, the lonely do have opportunities which they might well grasp with grateful hands.

One of the British Broadcasting Corporation's longest-lived programmes, which capitalizes this theme by supposing various celebrities cast off upon a desert island, frequently explores the subject's reaction to loneliness. A surprising number, mainly from the more gregarious and public sections of society, express a modified pleasure at the prospect. Many at any rate persuade themselves that they would find positive enjoyment in seclusion and privacy—for a limited time!

This is not merely to echo Scott's "a wise man is never less alone than when he is alone", or Sir Philip Sidney's sententious "they are never alone that are accompanied with noble thoughts". Though it is perfectly true, and no small part of the modern problem, that rich natures can stand loneliness as shallow ones can not. But there is more to it than that.

III

There is a loneliness which is the very condition of greatness; a loneliness without which excellence in any realm is impossible. There is, too, the loneliness demanded by great courage; and the loneliness of conscience without which great character is impossible; and the loneliness of leadership, of consecration, and of sacrifice. The dread of being found believing what only few believe, of behaving as only few think right, is craven: it forgets that the whole hope of humanity lies—under God—in its pioneering minorities, so often created and inspired by the single, lonely soul. The gibe that America is the land of freedom, where everyone is at liberty to do what everyone else is doing, may be grossly unfair, but it barbs a truth. Of course, he who chooses to stand alone when he need not is foolish and arrogant: but he who will not when he should is a coward and a slave.

And there is the overriding opportunity of the uncrowded life, that one can know the fellowship of the Most High as hearts without solitude can never do. Elizabeth Fry, in the midst of her utterly busy and over-peopled life, yearned often for "the mental and spiritual *stretch*" of being alone. We know what she means, and beside that spiritual stretch we may set that *sincerity* which Jesus held proved when prayer, and almsgiving, and fasting were pursued in the secret place. All experience of God has individual roots. In our admiration for vast religious assemblies and our passion for spiritual statistics we frequently forget how God needed to get His men alone to deal with them—from Abraham and Jacob, Moses in the wilderness and on the mount, Joshua at Jericho and Gideon behind the winepress, to John in the desert, to Paul's virtually unshared experience at Damascus, and to another John on Patmos. Man's loneliness is so often God's opportunity.

Inevitably we remember Jesus: the lonely nights of prayer, the early morning solitude, the unshared responsibility among crowds in Galilee, the growing isolation among critics in Judea;

we recall the wish for company in Gethsemane, that was denied Him, and the forsaking at His trial and His cross; we cannot forget the awful last loneliness of the dreadful cry, "My God, my God, why hast Thou forsaken me?" With Alice Meynell we remember that

> Public was death; but power, but might,
>   But life again, but victory,
> Were hushed within the dead of night,
>   The shuttered dark, the secrecy,
> And all alone, alone, alone,
> He rose again behind the stone.

Here in perfection is the loneliness of character, of courage, of consecration and leadership and sacrifice: yet within it is the constant awareness of divine companionship. "The Father is with me . . . He who sent me is with me, He has not left me alone."

IV

But of course this loneliness is only partial. It has God, and faith, and fellowship, within it. "Religion," said a great philosopher, "is what you do with your solitariness"—an aphorism which sounds even better the other way round: "What one does with solitariness is—religion!"

At any rate it is the Christian religion. For Jesus came to the desolate with a call into fellowship—"the fellowship of the Son of God's love". He sought out the lonely: the woman coming alone to draw water, the blind man avoiding crowds in the city, Zaccheus the ostracized, the leper debarred from all society, the one man left at the Pool of Siloam, the grieving Peter; and the promise "I will not leave you desolate" is for all whose lives have fallen in solitary places. The more that He Himself was rejected and thrust out and forced to stand and suffer alone, the more He strove to bind His men in loyalty and fellowship, in service and a remembering Communion that should make the Church one through all generations. And His final, unforgettable words were on this theme: "Lo, I am with you—always."

V

For the ultimate, inescapable truth is, that human experience knows no social cement, no creative fellowship, no motive force making for solidarity and sympathy and true community, to compare with the Christian faith. It could not be otherwise. A religion which assumes the divine family as its deepest faith, which proclaims reconciliation as its God-given message, which demands unlimited love as its final and sufficient law, and which looks towards a kingdom as its consummating hope, can only be individualistic and divisive by contradicting itself. Each of these foci of the Christian faith presupposes and creates community: and the supreme, uncounterfeited expression of the genius of Christianity is "koinonia"—the deeply-rooted, far-out-reaching fellowship of hearts made one in love of Christ.

Without such transcendent impulse towards cohesiveness and understanding, human society impelled by self-interest, competitiveness, rivalry, and mutual fear, *must* fall apart. The rat-race struggle for existence eliminates the unaggressive, the altruistic, and the submissive, as well as the unfit: only a Christian valuation of each other erects the refuge of justice, charity, and concern and offers to hearts otherwise lonely, unsheltered and exposed a love like God's to assuage their solitude.

And when godly people can do no more, still God Himself is near. Says Paul of the last stages of his trial: "No one took my part; all deserted me. . . . But the Lord stood by me." Said the psalmist of some more personal desolation: "My father and my mother have forsaken me, but the Lord will take me up." Says God to His people on the threshold of Canaan, and again in the years of Babylonian exile, and yet again in days of threatening persecution: "I will be with thee: I will not fail thee nor forsake."

3

Never was loneliness more keen than that of two who walked immeasurably bereaved through a world of gathering darkness to a lonely village home and an empty morrow—but "Jesus himself drew near and went with them."

With Him for company, even loneliness becomes a means of grace.

5

FAITHLESSNESS

I

"AND WHAT did you learn today?" asked the inevitably fond mother of the most diminutive and precocious junior who ever attended school. "Not much," was the superb reply, "all about sums and God."

To span thus early, and in one day, the extremes of human knowledge, must be unique. For "sums" is the one-syllable epitome of all scientific measurement and comprehension of the world around us, even as the word "God" summarizes all human insight and conviction concerning the mysterious world within. And at both extremes, though he did not know it, junior—like the rest of us—was learning to apprehend by *faith*.

For the boundaries of human certainty are strictly limited. Crawling into an oven on a cold day, one of Europe's greatest thinkers emerged after many hours with warmed feet and a new system of philosophy, of which the foundation truth was "I think—therefore I am." All else, he argued, was doubtful—the existence of the body, of the oven, of any real world behind my sense experience, the existence of other minds, in other bodies, which are only colours and sounds in my mind. Only one thing I know, that I think, and therefore must exist. The rest is argument.

Descartes might have got even colder feet had his logic been more strict. "I think, therefore I am" makes an enormous unproved assumption about existence. Even the more accurate "I think, therefore I think" assumes a continuity in time which cannot be proved. All the philosopher really cooked up that chilly day was the bare certainty, "I think, therefore I thought!"

II

All this seems nonsense to normal people, who take the world and themselves for granted. But it is not at all nonsense to remember that *all* man's knowledge consists of logical constructions built up step by step from facts and truths that cannot be proved but only "seen" by inspection. At the very outset of discovery *we have to trust* our senses, and believe that the world we think we see, is so. Then, by a further *act of faith*, we believe in our own powers of deduction: if we cannot "see" how one step implies another, nothing will prove it to us. All knowledge begins with unsupported faith—in human observation and human reason.

This complete intellectual dependence upon unprovable intuition is much more obvious when we are dealing with questions of beauty, or value, of right or wrong. All explanations ended, a man must "see for himself" where beauty and goodness lie. He must trust his own perception of aesthetic excellence and moral obligation, just as he does of intellectual truth: or remain in utter ignorance. And confidence in one's intuitive perceptions is in fact the essence of faith.

Some who disdain religious faith as wishful thinking and comfortable make-believe, conveniently forget that it is only the application to wider realms of a power native to the human mind and necessary to all intellectual activity.

III

But religious faith is an infinitely richer thing than this commonplace trust in our own processes of knowledge. Following the clues of history and experience, reinforced by its success in other realms of knowledge, strengthened by the testimony of the good and great in all ages, and especially by the flood of light and understanding that streams from Christ, faith reaches out to grasp heaven by the hems, and holds traffic already among eternal things.

So immeasurably rewarding has this exercise proved, that it might almost be said to be *the* religious attitude to life and to the world. One whose situation demanded faith in unique degree, not only to make any achievement possible but to make existence itself tolerable—Miss Helen Keller, blind, deaf, and dumb since infancy—defined faith as "an indivisible totality of beliefs that inspire", adding with rare authority: "Faith reinvigorates the will, enriches the affections, and awakens a sense of creativeness."

This power is demonstrated in the roll of outstanding figures in Israelite history who are cited as heroes of faith, men of immense responsibility, who shaped generations, determined events, and stood in the main stream of world development. It is striking that each was tempted to shrink from responsibility and take refuge in his own littleness: Moses crying "Not I . . .", Joshua needing repeated encouragement, Gideon hanging his head behind the winepress, Saul hiding among the baggage, Jeremiah pleading his youth, until faith matched each for his time and duty.

For faith is the alternative, not to reason, but to self-depreciation, and to scepticism towards life: nothing cripples or inhibits like want of faith in the worthwhileness of struggle and the certainty of true reward. Great faith is the spring of great effort, and to lack it is to limit all human endeavour.

IV

Nazareth has a twofold title to fame in biblical history: it nurtured Him who was the Champion and the Exemplar and the Object of the life of faith, and it rendered Him comparatively helpless by its obdurate unbelief. Mark says Jesus *could* do no mighty work there, as though He were hampered; Matthew says He *did* none, as though it were a judgement on Nazareth's faithlessness: and both are true. So the faithless village takes its place beside the faithless generation that under Moses reached the borders of the promised land and failed to enter in "because of unbelief".

Great opportunities are often thrown away because the heart is sceptical of fine things ever coming to pass, and refuses to commit itself to great hopes for fear of greater disappointment. But faith is the alternative to fear: as the undiscourageable expectation of good, it will not let Canaan go, will not let Christ pass by. It nurses the invincible conviction that what is right can be done, what is good can be achieved—with God.

In this respect faith is manifested as a reasoned belief in the incredible, that attacks the impossible with courage and un-flagging hope. It grasps each great opportunity because it cannot forget the words of Jesus: "All things are possible to him who believes." Whether it be a mountain to be removed, the pro-verbial metaphor for seemingly insuperable obstacles which faith surmounts; or a deep-rooted sycamore to be plucked from its place and replanted in the sea, a vivid picture of faith tackling the unthinkable and winning through; in either case, to face the impossible with God, *and in His will*, is to face it triumphantly.

Another gospel incident illumines faith's relevance to human relationships. Listening to Jesus talking about forgiveness—unlimited, generous, free, repeated as oft as your brother repents—the Apostles were astonished at such demands upon human patience, and expostulated "Lord, increase our *faith*!"

The unexpected insight is true. Faith in God, and in man, and in man's capacity for moral improvement, is essential to that magnanimity which Sir Charles Snow has suggested is dying out of modern life. One only really forgives an injury suffered if one truly believes in the repentance of the wrongdoer, and in the possibility of creating a new, redemptive situation by a generous act of pardon. Here the alternative to faith is not reason but cynicism, that thinks no good of its neighbour, that explains away all his efforts at reform, and leaves no opportunity for new beginnings. Human relations are embittered, and the vicious circle of wrong heaped on wrong spins all the faster as faith fades: for only faith keeps open the door to change, and summons to its aid powers not of man's kindling to reclaim a brother.

v

"By faith we understand"—for faith is the light of the Christian intelligence, and its alternative is superstition, always the nemesis of unbelief. By faith we "stand" (as Paul told the Corinthians)— for faith is the nerve of the Christian conscience; "in nothing affrighted" it knows itself kept by the power of God. By faith we "live" (as the prophet declared)—for faith is the spring of Christian endurance, standing on its watchtower in dark and perplexing days and holding on, in spite of all appearances, to the justice and mercy of God. By faith we are "saved" (as the whole New Testament affirms)—for faith is the channel of divine energies that regenerate, rekindle, and redeem.

We affirm, then, faith's intellectual necessity, its spiritual insight, its inspiration and energy, its grasp of opportunity, its confidence in life and in all things good, its creative and healing influence in human relationships, its sustaining and redemptive power in spiritual experience—a considerable claim. But all this is possible only because in Christian thought, faith has its anchorage in God. "Have faith," says Jesus, "*in God.*" Never less than that.

Walt Whitman's meditation on the "noiseless, patient spider", unreeling across a gap the floating filament of web until a waving strand shall find its hold and bridge the gulf—

> And you, O my soul, where you stand
> Surrounded, detached in measureless oceans of space
> Ceaselessly musing, venturing, throwing, seeking the spheres to
>   connect them

Till the bridge you need be formed, till the ductile anchor hold,
Till the gossamer thread you fling catches somewhere, O my soul . . .

elaborates an evocative metaphor, but it leaves faith hanging precariously in the air. The marvel, the miracle, of Christian faith's endeavour, enrichment, and endurance is explained because faith is the open door through which the living God invades the life, the link between two worlds, the bond between two personalities, human and divine. Faith is a relationship; not seeking only, or believing, or aspiring, or hoping, or gathering one's moral resources in a mighty resolve, but an "I—Thou" experience of divine Reality, an existential encounter with the living God. Faith makes God a man's companion, and in divine company, power, understanding, strength, endurance, achievement are all made possible.

VI

But the climate of the twentieth century has not hitherto been congenial to the development of deep faith. Scientific achievement tends to pride and self-reliance, although the secrets we explore are secrets God wrought, and the outcome of our knowledge has proved a perilously mixed blessing. Affluence tends to independence and self-sufficiency, and we miss the elementary lessons in the life of faith that hardship, struggle and adversity so eloquently teach. Materialism, too, fascinates the gaze with an abundance of secular "consumables" that stifle the hunger that might remind us of the soul's infinity.

Yet these things begin to pall. Fear, confusion, superstition, and despair, scepticism towards the future, cynicism towards men and continual belittlement of human life are no sustaining diet for the spirit of man. The heart cries out for something to believe in, greatly and commandingly. Man may drag out a dull existence in his little self-made prison of denial and proud doubt: but he will not *live*—nobly, profitably, enjoyably, or hopefully—

without faith, a steady confidence in his own spiritual intuitions about life, the world and himself, and a committed, personalized trust in One who, knowing the spirit of man and the height and depth of human experience, bade us have faith in God.

*"Those who belong to Christ Jesus have
crucified the flesh with its passions and
desires."*   Galatians 5:24

6

LASCIVIOUSNESS

I

OUR THEME is repellent; its discussion will be distasteful.
Yet in preaching for today it would be cowardice to evade
its terrible relevance.

For it is a characteristic of post-war Western society that a
sentimental romanticism which was never sufficiently realistic
about love and marriage is giving place to a sensual realism which
despises romance. The cult of "naturism" is descending, by its
own corrupting logic, to the most unnatural exaggerations and
perversions of human desire. Human love, which should be
youth's inspiration and delight, is fast becoming sullied, commercialized, degraded, by an eroticism that identifies living with
loving and loving with sex in its least exalted, entirely physical,
expression.

Pornographic films, books, plays and perversions are part of
the social common market of Europe, and America, so long the
centre of the new entertainment-culture, and pace-setter in every
rebellion against inhibitions, censorship, and convention, is
certainly not exempt. Throughout the West, a flood of sex-
glorifying paperbacks covers the bookstalls with erotic symbols
and slogans, while the theatre and the novel have descended from
the "working class" home to the slum, from the "homely"
kitchen to the kitchen sink and on to the lavatory, for their all-
too-appropriate setting.

The British Press Council "as the first thing it did, proclaimed itself deeply disturbed by the unwholesome exploitation of sex by certain newspapers and periodicals", and a leading United States evangelical magazine has in recent years regularly called attention to "unassailable evidence that many television and radio programmes, many movies, the misnamed 'comics', and the filthy literature sold at the average news stand and bookstore all portray crime, violence, lust and evil in general in ways that glorify and glamorize sin." A shameless agitation proceeds for social approval of homosexual perversions as, first of all a psychological misfortune, and later as the "daring" credentials of a select and sophisticated coterie of "progressive" intellectuals.

Intellectual and illiterate here join hands. On one side, thousands of pounds are invested by "reputable" firms in purveying near-pornographic literature and films, and skilled advocates, for high fees, defend the trade in filth as the hallmark of an "adult" society expressing its maturity and freedom. On the other side, morally indistinguishable in the level of enjoyment, is the back-street printer and the carefully secluded bookstall turning out mental dirt for weak-minded and sadistic adolescents to wallow in sexual exhibitionism, sniggering eroticism, and the cult of phallic love.

The results of this lucrative trade in sensuality are becoming obvious. The British Medical Association expresses serious concern over the number of illegitimate children born to early-teen-age mothers (one Church Welfare Department alone reports a one-third increase in one year), and over the general promiscuity prevalent among young adolescents. A heart-aching study by Mrs. Lynne Gladstone Millar incorporated revealing facts and opinions supplied by schoolchildren themselves. Increasing assaults, even upon very young girls, and boys, are a feature of city life in most Western lands, and a rash of furtive clubs and "theatres" for the exploitation and enjoyment of vice disfigures most great centres of population. The Mother of Parliaments herself explicitly refused to interfere with London's strip-tease industry.

It is the deserted home, the parentless, loveless babe, the diseased and demented adolescent, the degraded woman and the raped child who pay for the intellectualist's boasted freedom, and who know the real extent of society's "maturity".

II

If the main concern is for youth, main responsibility is unquestionably with age. "These are the children of our society," says one responsible report on the teen-age sexual situation; "moulded by our society, by parents, teachers, entertainers, by the Church, by the highbrow triflers with sex as well as by the lowbrow and commercial exploiters of it." Corrupted adolescents, says another authority, "were victims of commercial exploitation by the papers they bought and the shows that were put before them, which exposed them to all manner of false suggestion." "The most important factor in this situation," says Lord Samuel, an outstanding British philosopher, scientist and Elder Statesman, "is the climate of public opinion, the tone of society. It is not only what kind of genes the individual is born with, but what kind of civilization he is born into, that . . . decides the development of his character."

This is not only true but frightening. As pernicious opinions and vicious practices are given increasing publicity, so the moral climate is accommodated, first to hearing of such things, then to tolerating them, and so to approving them, if only by silence, lest protest be scorned as outmoded and priggish. Two perceptive and courageous journalists, arguing the responsibility of the press for much of the morbid interest in—and imitation of—crimes of violence, show how the press can appear as guardians of social values while at the same time covertly offering the satisfaction of reading titillating material; the reader is encouraged to retain his sense of moral indignation while reading things that decent and sensitive minds refuse to contemplate.

This process of the social habilitation of lust has two

distinguishable stages. The first is the assumed attitude of neutrality, the observer not presuming to express a moral judgement. Films demonstrate immoral behaviour, "mirroring life", without comment and carefully concealing consequences: "they show how others do these things". A glaring example of this deliberate advertisement by detached reporting, was an interview with a strip-tease "artiste" broadcast by the British Broadcasting Corporation in—above all things—"Woman's Hour", thereby adding insult to indecency. Some "factual" sociological press articles similarly evade the responsibility of moral assessment while surreptitiously helping to create a climate in which immorality becomes a matter of absorbing interest.

The sensational, the outrageous, is irresistible as circulation-fodder. The rebels, the undisciplined, the perverted, get exaggerated notice just because they are untypical, and by implication the responsible and disciplined and wholesome are represented as "square", negative, and dull. When to this artificially heightened interest in immorality is added the pose of moral indifference disguised as "adult, broad-minded toleration", the result is more insidiously corrupting than outright approval would be.

III

The second stage in this process is the argument that a man's private morality is entirely his own affair, exempt from criticism, from obligation, and from morality. If lust, fornication, homosexual perversions, are branded in religious eyes as *sins*, yet "sin is no crime", and the individual is free to pursue his private lusts unhindered and uncondemned. Those whose profitable business is to purvey pornographic literature, drugs, alcohol, and prostitution are but faithfully fulfilling a public need, and are benefactors of society.

To this, the first answer is, that no man's inner life is ever kept private, and it would offer no opportunity for commercial exploitation if it were. Secret indulgence is reflected, inevitably, in all a man does and is, as parent, neighbour, citizen. Character is the slow deposit of the hidden tides of thought, imagination, and desire—and no man liveth to himself. For this reason, the privately vicious are always a public menace.

Secondly, the slogan "sin is no crime" forgets the only basis of social law, in the private conscience of individuals. Society itself has no right to enforce conformity with its will, or to punish deviations, except as that will is seen to be *right*. Otherwise law is simply the bullying of the majority. Sometimes a public enactment is so obviously out of touch with the moral sense of the majority that its provisions are widely ignored, and ridiculed: without the assent of the private conscience, law is ultimately powerless. The same principle underlies the jury system, the common law, and every appeal to the authority of Crown or People. To divorce the standards of public morals and crime, therefore, from the private opinions of most citizens as to what constitutes an evil, a sin by impartial and absolute standards, is in the end to undermine social order and bring law itself into contempt.

"Sin is no crime" is the motto of a confessedly godless society, explicitly affirming that its public standards have no superhuman reference or source. Biblical religion vehemently and persistently protests against this separation of the religious consciousness from social righteousness and public welfare: law, prophets, and Jesus alike assert the divine will over home and market-place, street and court, inner and outer life. Most of the Sermon on the Mount is in fact the elaboration of this theme, that a tree privately rotten cannot produce public fruit of any value; that where men decay, the State is poisoned. It is interesting how very often an "advanced" irreligious view is really a return to positions—in this case, the separation of religion from righteousness—which religion itself abandoned long ago.

IV

Argument, however, is not enough. The recent accelerated trend towards lasciviousness and licence must be met also with compassion, and resistance. An American observer, analysing shrewdly the price youth pays for mental indiscipline, mentions a premature ageing of the flesh and spirit which robs of true vitality, adding that experiences purely physical in character impoverish and bankrupt life, with eventual feelings of failure and frustration. Disorderly and frantic pseudo-love destroys the delicate balance between what is naturally sexual and what is spiritual and idealistic in married love, and the highest experience of complete mutual joy is rendered impossible.

That is well said. When to this psychological impoverishment is added the emotional confusion, the embitterment of affections, which inevitably follow upon undisciplined lust; the harvest of heartache, loneliness, disillusion, and emotional despair that is sown; the moral enfeeblement that seeping through the whole character undermines mind and will and personality; the marriages vitiated at the outset by soiled conceptions of sexual relationship, by animal selfishness unrefined by tenderness, by ruthless hedonism unrestrained by responsibility; and the sociological problems multiplying through such domestic backgrounds for the next generation—it is obvious that condemnation without compassion for the immeasurable loss youth suffers would be heartless.

We should add to the toll the religious insensibility that sensualism invariably breeds. To be young is glorious: but our cynicism, sophistries, and sins, have made our modern world a fearfully difficult place in which to be young and good.

This is where compassion toward the young evokes anger toward our hypocritical society. A generation without beliefs, without standards, without loyalties, without self-discipline in its own entertainments, literature, and life, has no right to moral indignation when it sees its own likeness mirrored in the rising generation. If it is ever to regain moral authority, and the respect of critical young hearts, society must curb its own excesses, punish heavily those who trade upon others' innocence or weakness, and reflect in its common life the standards it desires youth to adopt.

V

Western society will do this only when a searching blast of essential ethical puritanism once more stirs the Church to confront an unbuttoned and lascivious decade with the holiness of God and the purity of Christ. The current situation calls for wholly new realism and frankness in the Church's training of its youth. It rebukes an evangelism more concerned with emotional experiences than with ethics and repentance. It challenges Christians to return to the towering ideal of personal holiness, and a more responsible share in the shaping of that public conscience from which our social codes arise. It cries aloud for the persistent proclamation of the redemptive and cleansing power of Christ in a decadent society, in the twentieth century as in the first.

Indeed, the moral climate of our time lends entirely new relevance to the evangelical message of the Cross, where Christ in spotless innocence bore the whole world's stain and sin, and in the body of His flesh through death redeemed the body itself from sin and death. Being identified by faith with all Christ did, Christians too have crucified the flesh with its passions and desires, putting to death the old self and rising to new life with Christ. Whoever kneels in penitence before the Cross of Jesus finds himself not only forgiven but liberated, renewed, and sanctified, and sent forth in the radiance of a cleansed heart, memory and imagination, and in the power of a Holy Spirit, to enjoy in uncorrupting happiness a victorious life in Christ.

7

DISINTEGRATION

I

IT IS curious that for modern minds the word "synthetic"
should have come to suggest something spurious, an "ersatz"
substitute-product, neither genuine nor wholesome. We are
more at home taking things to pieces, and tend to suspect any
compounding things together as artificial, and false.

This odd suspicion crystallizes one widespread difference
between our own and certain earlier ages. For "synthesis" was
formerly the aim of philosopher after philosopher, and the
"synoptic" view, seeing life steadily and seeing it whole, was an
accepted mark of the educated mind. Trying for a comprehensive
viewpoint, from which everything would appear orderly,
coherent, and meaningful, was once a powerful motive of
religious thought, and the confidence that in spite of all appearances the totality of things was in fact one, a universe, was a
prime article of religious faith.

The revered author of *The Philosophy of Civilisation* has
declared that ours is "an age which is devoid of a philosophic
survey of the world as a whole". But we scarcely needed to be
told. For us, all synthesis, all "total views", are suspect; analysis
is the accepted "scientific" method. We love to break down the
complex into its constituents; the universe to its elements, the
elements to atoms, the atoms to electrons, protons, mesons; and
the mind likewise into its constituent strata—conscious, subconscious, unconscious, racial, "chemical" elements, and so on.
This is our intellectual mood, a breaking down in order to

49   4

understand. Sometimes we find we have broken down merely to destroy.

The range of this modern preoccupation with splitting things up is astonishing. Almost every modern trend, almost every fashionable habit, contributes to a frenzy of fragmentation, tending to obscure life's essential unity, to dissolve social cohesiveness, to leave only bits and pieces of experience that we find desperately hard to fit back together into any ordered pattern. Henry Miller, a leader of American "new-thinkers", is reported as saying: "Long ago . . . I was revelling in the fact that the world about me was going to pieces. Indeed from the time I was old enough to think for myself, I was convinced of this. . . . Nor did I have the cheek then to say, as Rimbaud did, 'as for me, I am intact!' It didn't matter to me whether I was intact or falling to pieces. I was assisting at a spectacle, the crumbling of our civilization . . ."

From a vastly different viewpoint, Paul Tillich has listed acutely the massed symptoms of this spiritual dissolution: "The disrupted, split, disintegrated personality, the hidden will to death, the torturing anxiety, the dread despair, the mental cleavage, the compulsions, neurotic trends, unconscious strivings, restlessness, which moves and whips us, unordered desires and hidden repressions . . . hostility against ourselves . . ."

This is the kind of fragmentation most vividly present to conscious life; what Lewis Mumford, in describing one of Joyce's characters, has called "living in a hell of unfulfilled desires, vague wishes, and enfeebling anxieties, morbid compulsions and dreary vacuities—a dissociated mind in a disintegrated city—perhaps the *normal* mind of the metropolis."

II

But this is, after all, only the reflection of a social environment in which the image of personality is everywhere broken up. The old moral pattern of life has been shattered. Whatever its faults, a rigid morality did hold life together within a framework of consistent and widely-held principles of conduct that gave society order and harmony. But one-sided emphasis upon individual freedom, upon the supposed dangers of repression, upon the variety and "artificiality" of the world's moral standards, has released disruptive forces of instinct, passion, selfishness, rebelliousness, that have created bewilderment, distraction, and paralysis of will, among the young, conflict between the generations, and cynicism and disillusion among the old, while society itself casts about to discover the authority and discipline it no longer possesses.

But modern thought, too, has fallen to pieces. A proliferation of sciences, each looking at part of life and often claiming to speak for the whole, has replaced the older attempts at synthesis. We lose all the threads; we believe a dozen contradictory theories; we sit open-mouthed at the feet of psychologist, geneticist, chemist, physicist, biologist, astronomer, logician, sociologist, historian in turn, and occasionally we like to set them at each other in some contentious quiz-team: and then go our way with a muddle of inconsistent "scientific" ideas at our command to justify anything we feel inclined to do or think.

Sir Julian Huxley, whose acquaintance with the many fields of modern knowledge is probably unrivalled, has recently stressed that the world's monster-problems "can only be successfully met in the light and with the aid of a new organization of thought and belief, a new dominant pattern of ideas. . . . If the situation is not to lead to chaos, despair, or escapism, man must reunify his life within the framework of a satisfactory idea-system . . . build a system of thought and belief which will provide both a supporting framework for his present existence, an ultimate or ideal goal for his future development as a species, and a guide and directive for practical action and planning." The intellectual problem of reintegration could hardly be stated with greater insight, or authority.

III

Moral and intellectual fragmentation are in turn reflected in the specialization that splits up man's work into a thousand separate skills and repetitive tasks, so that few any longer make any whole thing but only the fraction of a fragment of a part of a thing, so dissipating the joy of creative craftsmanship and reducing labour to drudgery.

Home, too, once the active centre of daily life, from which a man went out to the world fortified, for which he worked in love, to which he returned to find sanctuary and strength, is being replaced by a multitude of commercialized eating-houses and sleeping-houses, where families rarely meet themselves. For that matter, the family itself is fast losing its natural unity, as the fever of specialization divides the unbroken stream of life into stylized age-groups, each with its own science, from paediatrics through pedagogy to psychiatry and geriatrics. And society, also, is fast becoming an aggregate of competing groups, age-groups, wage-groups, pressure-, cultural-, political-groups, rather than a living organism whose constituent parts have in a few limited respects a diversity of interests and functions.

Even the Church has not escaped the contagion of schizophrenia: for upon the intractable divisions which history and divergences of interpretation have imposed, the twentieth-century Church has added an astonishing multiplicity of age and interest and cultural and functional separations, until in many instances the local "Church" is little more than the sum total of the multifarious societies and organizations that happen to meet in the parent premises.

It is all painfully familiar; to psychiatrists, social workers, and all friends of youth, it is all too obviously impoverishing, disruptive, and perilous. In reaction, some seek the security of a strictly imposed discipline, placing themselves unreservedly under a pattern of life designed by authoritarian order, surrendering all initiative and with it all responsibility, to the ordained Rule. Others justify fragmentation of life by an "existentialist" philosophy that denies the significance of unity, pattern, and order altogether, and lives for the moment as it comes, undisciplined and undirected because unmeaning. Many again simply departmentalize conduct and thought, and pursue in many selves a dissociated, vulnerable and inconsistent life of uneasy accommodation. In earnest souls, an unresolved spiritual conflict proceeds through alternate victory and despair that often breaks into Paul's heartfelt cry, "Wretched man that I am! Who will deliver me . . .?"

IV

The Christian answer to that cry is expressed in a dozen phrases where the characteristic New Testament word for "salvation" is, on stricter interpretation, "healthiness, soundness, wholeness". The maimed, whose paralysed limbs have robbed life of some part of its completeness, are "made whole". Faith "makes whole" the life shattered and diminished by sin. "They that are whole" need no physician, but many are sick—incompletely alive, lacking some part of that fullness of life which Jesus came to bestow.

Jesus well knew that mental and moral schizophrenia is painful, weakening, unstable, disastrous. No "house" divided against itself can stand, whether it be the house of the soul, of the family, or of society. And His question to men, to families and to society, is still that which, in the idiom of the older version, He put to the man at the Pool of Bethesda: "Wilt thou be made whole?" An apt comment comes from "a well-known medical psychologist" (and the professionally anonymous phrase here covers ample authority): "I believe that the way of life presented by the Christian ethic offers us the highest in the realm of the Spirit. If this were applied to what we already know about the mind and body, we, as physicians and priests, would soon help to bring about such a wholeness of man as has never been known . . ."

It is plainly no accident that one of the loftiest statements of the purpose of Christ is framed in just such terms: "a plan for the fullness of time, to unite all things in Him, things in heaven and things on earth"; or, in another New Testament passage, we read it pleased God "through Him to reconcile to Himself all things, whether on earth or in heaven." The social effect of Christ in the first century and in every century since has been to draw men to Himself, and so to one another: to dispel isolation, break down walls of partition, and create out of Jew, Greek, Barbarian, bond and free, male and female, one communion, "all one in Christ Jesus".

And in the individual soul likewise, the work of Christ is to unify, integrate, reconcile, gathering into one pattern of moral strength and beauty the various impulses, drives, and aspirations within each personality. Surrender to His direction, love for His person, devotion for His cause, wonderfully unite the heart.

v

Of course the Christian mind must still wrestle with the multitudinous themes and insights of modern knowledge, and will frequently be overwhelmed with the sheer variety and excitement of discovery, the immense vistas of still unanswered questions that beckon his curiosity. Yet having learned the key to life's maze "as the truth is in Jesus" he will possess a unifying faith, and find that wherever new knowledge touches upon conduct and human experience it falls into place within the Christian scheme, illumined still further by the mind of the Master and contributing always to that total truth which is the thought of God.

Of course too the Christian heart will wrestle with conflicting emotional and temperamental trends within himself, and against the pressures and enticements of the world outside: yet here again, the unifying discipline of a worshipped ideal, a welcome and beloved Mastering, will sustain the pattern after which character is being moulded, and hold the Christian life to its integrating purpose by loyalty to Jesus.

By the expulsive power of a great passion for Christ, by the subduing power of an unpayable debt to Christ, by the illuminating power of a faith centred upon Christ, by the kindling and renewing power of Christ's immaculate example, harmony is established in believing hearts from within, and life finds its focus, its framework, its foundation, and its final goal, in the love of Christ. In Him life becomes reintegrated, the heart united, our aims are unified, our thought is made coherent: to us also He will say, Thy faith hath made thee whole.

8

HUMANISM

I

"ANYONE can create a new religion," says John Watson; "all he needs is self-confidence and a supply of foolscap." Neither is in short supply, and it is not surprising therefore that our scientific humanists, who until recently were debunking religion as a mere "insurance policy from the universe", as "the happiness of credulity", "weak fancies and dramatizations of reality", "a dangerous venture into the field of ultimate metaphysics in quest of cosmic alliance and support", should now be busy reconstructing a religion of their own.

No rational man, with sensitive conscience and warm affections, can be content to live in a world whose origin is accident and in which reason, sanity, love, and moral purpose have no rightful home. An idiot world frightens us, frustrates, infuriates, and offends us. At the very least the heart still sighs for the splendours of the lost beliefs: agnosticism possesses little excitement, inspiration, or glory! The pretence that those who relinquish religion are relieved of a great burden is itself sheer wishful thinking.

There is more at stake, however, than the heart's hunger for joy. "One of the main things needed by the world today," says Sir Julian Huxley—of all people—"is a new single religious system . . . not merely a rationalist denial of the old but a religious affirmation of something new. . . . All religions are psychosocial organs of evolving man: their function is to help him to cope with the problems of his destiny."

This view is a positive advance upon the same writer's earlier estimate of religion: "A little of the best side of the religious spirit is like salt in cooking—it improves most things. . . . God is a necessary and fruitful creation of the human soul." These more patronizing valuations echo Gibbon's dictum: "All religions are considered by the people as equally true, by the philosophers as equally false, and by the magistrates as equally valuable." They recall too the words of Aldous Huxley: "It was fashionable during the Enlightenment of the middle nineteenth century to speak of the need of supplying the masses with 'vital lies' calculated to make those who accepted them not only happy but well behaved." Voltaire, in the same spirit, is supposed to have silenced his sophisticated friends while the servant was in the room, because if scepticism spread to the lower orders "neither our lives nor our property would be safe".

Such cynicism is an inverted testimony to the fact that "religion has been responsible for a good deal of social and individual good". Jung's famous remark, "Among my patients in the second half of life, that is over thirty-five, there has not been one whose problem in the last resort was not that of finding a religious outlook" may be paralleled with another, expressing his apprehension that if Christianity be doomed with the advance of knowledge to disappear, "a frenzy of demoralization will sweep over humanity".

Man can hardly avoid "busying himself with all reverence with his ultimate destiny in the universe". Religious experiences have to be reckoned among the facts with which science has to deal, and some psychologists who deny the truth of religion nevertheless appreciate, and try to conserve, its psychological value. D. S. Cairns asserts the moral argument for religion: "The average mind of western Christendom today tends to accept the scientific view of the world as the ultimate truth about it, while at the same time all the better spirits desire to conserve as much of the Christian values, especially the valuation of man, as is believed to be possible." And Sir Julian Huxley adds an aesthetic consideration: maintaining vigorously his opposition to theistic belief he acknowledges the value that lies "in the tradition of religion, the hallowed beauty of the buildings and the solace of religious service".

Such are the reasons behind what T. S. Eliot called the "rush of scientists to stake out a little quasi-religious territory for themselves". It is not surprising that a religion constructed on these rationalistic and utilitarian grounds should fashion its god in man's own image. All idols are projections of man's inner self, and a man-made god is the only deity which preserves man's sovereignty and pride.

It is the cardinal faith of humanism that "the forces needed for redemption and for the ennobling of life are to be found within man", that within man there is that which once set free from unfavourable circumstances has the power to rise to a new and more splendid social order. "Human control by human effort in accordance with human ideals" is humanism's watchword and its hope.

No one who believes in incarnation will challenge the humanist statement that "the spiritual elements which are usually called divine are part and parcel of human nature, and the highest flights of the human spirit are as much realities as the routine activities of the human body". When this high estimate of man is carried still further: "So far as we know, man is the highest type of individual in existence, and if therefore there is any proper object of religious devotion, a 'real' god, it can only be humanity considered in its noblest aspirations and capacities, together with nature so far as expressed in and serviceable to humanity"—we confront a "deification of man by man" which is plainly hollow, rhetorical, and self-deceiving. Yet it is at least refreshing in these days to meet a valuation of man that rescues him from the primeval slime and the ultimate atomic dust and accords him some spirituality of nature and some dignity of reverence.

On the lowest, materialistic, terms man is remarkable. In the average human brain there are as many separate living cells as there are stars in the Milky Way—some ten thousand million. That coincidental correspondence is somehow symbolic of the amazing power of the human mind to apprehend the fathomless splendours of the universe. When to these facts is added man's self-consciousness, and his capacity for appreciation, valuation, and reverence, it is plain the Bible does not idly claim he is the crown of all creation. That is the truth in humanism.

II

For all that, a man-made religion of which man himself is the supreme deity must fail. Its emergence underlines the moral, social and psychological necessity of *some* religion, the insatiable spiritual hunger in the heart of man, and man's sense of superiority over all material things. But it emphasizes no less that self-made religion is no religion at all.

Religion without revelation must be a religion without devotion: we cannot really worship ourselves—we know ourselves too well. We cannot abase ourselves before the work of our own hands, or the conceptions of our own minds. Pride, self-will and all aggressiveness are not merely tolerated but sanctified in such humanistic religiousness. With the record of the twentieth century vividly in mind it is futile to ask modern men to place their trust in men—either princes, philosophers, or scientists. "Few pages are more tragic or . . . more grotesque," writes Professor De Burgh, "than those which record the effort of civilized Europe during the last two centuries to wrest the idea of humanity from its other-worldly foundations and to base a humanistic gospel on the progress of civilization and the perfectibility of human nature."

The progress of civilization is far from obvious. "What science has done hitherto is to improve the means for achieving un-improved or actually deteriorated ends" is Aldous Huxley's terrible judgement. "Man who at one time dreamt of himself as a little lower than the angels, has submitted to become the servant and minister of nature," said Whitehead. Servitude to nature usually spells disorder and misery to man, and in fact man has become not only servant but victim. For the price of man's new knowledge of nature has proved to be the imminent peril of his own destruction.

Man cannot lose faith in himself and worship himself at the same time. Where there is neither worship, abasement, trust nor faith, there is scarcely religion!

But the truth is, humanism always dehumanizes man. As Maritain has said, "To offer man only what is human is to betray him . . . for by the principal part of him, which is the mind, man is called to something better than a purely human life."

Berdyaev has stated this succinctly. "Human life becomes truly terrible when there ceases to be anything above man." This is confirmed by familiar descriptions of contemporary Western society, its fearful uniformity, its megalopolitan culture, its vast cities breeding an irrational, depersonalized atmosphere, the "deep spiritual solitude of modern man", "the state of spiritual desolation in which contemporary humanity finds itself".

However we explain it, one result of humanism has been to depress human worth, to iron out individuality, to make the human spirit sterile, to level human experience to the mudflats of time and bound human existence by the darkness of the grave.

III

The third failure of humanistic religion follows from this. One cannot derive man from the animals, and so by popular implication equate man with the animals, without encouraging animality in man to the exclusion of that which is divine. It is the sorry experience of mankind that ape and angel divide the empire of Mansoul: if the angel be declared illusory, the ape reigns unopposed.

One expects therefore that in the context of humanist denials and wholly naturalistic science, light talk of free love and outmoded moralities should find congenial company; that the enjoyment of sensation for its own sake, heightened and intoxicated by drugs and by artificial stimulants of all kinds, and pursued into all manner of perversions and exaggerations, should be advocated as the normal man's "natural" reaction to the dilemma of existence.

For humanistic religion cannot discipline human nature. Man worshipping himself will soon excuse, then justify, and finally canonize his sins. A repeated misprint in a recent humanist symposium cites Sir Julian Huxley's book as "Religion without Revolution"—an error which speaks volumes. Humanistic religion offers no hope at all to the defeated, the sinful, the lost.

Nor, finally, can humanistic religion offer consolation or courage. It is fair criticism: for the new scientific "faith", if it is to replace the old, must show its power to accomplish more adequately what the older faith achieved. It can do nothing of the kind. Humanistic religion is, at best, a "faith" for men sheltered from life's poverty, pain, and bitterness, from tragedy and fear; a university product for the university campus, which may be transplanted to the drawing-rooms of the cultivated and protected mentors of an affluent society but will scarcely survive in the slums of the great cities, in the wards of incurable agony, on the battlefield, or in any situation where human hearts are brought to breaking point.

W. S. Urquhart could say twenty years ago that "the darkness has grown deeper, the tragedy of human helplessness and the injustice of things is more keenly felt, and revolt is overshadowed by despair". In reply to this we are offered "Stoicism in plus-fours", "the high religion of the twentieth century"—"to discipline ourselves to desire only what is possible, think only mortal thoughts, awake to the limits of man's capacity and accept it with tranquil resignation".

It will not do. The "firm foundation of unyielding despair" is still despair, and the human heart cries out for consolation, and for hope. Cries out in fact for a faith whose Deity is not wilfully fashioned by man in man's own image, but Who willingly and in love became man, to share man's life and suffering, to taste—and conquer—death for every man. Such a holy, transcendent, love *compels* worship, exalts humanity, creates and imposes its own moral discipline, and nourishes within the heart such courage and hope as the world finds nowhere else.

In face of man's predicament, self-confidence and foolscap are not enough. When someone said he had invented a religion superior to any other but did not know how to launch it upon the world, Talleyrand replied: "Go and be crucified, and in three days rise again. That is the way to launch a religion."

It is indeed. Hear Edward Shillito:

> If we have never sought, we seek Thee now;
>   Thine eyes burn through the dark, our only stars;
> We must have sight of thorn-pricks on Thy brow,
>   We must have Thee, O Jesus of the scars.
>
> The heavens frighten us; they are too calm;
>   In all the universe we have no place.
> Our wounds are hurting us . . .
>
> But to our wounds only God's wounds can speak,
>   And not a god has wounds, but Thou alone.

9

TRANSIENCE

I

YOUTH is for dreams, romance, and high adventure; for fun and fickleness and long, long thoughts; for great attempting and divine impatience. Few things spotlight the *malaise* of the modern Western world more poignantly than the conviction of young minds that life will be brief, its years overshadowed, its end unimaginably violent—"so what the hell?"

To be sure, this is not the universal reaction. That it is possible, even to twenty-five per cent of those who stand at the threshold of adult life, is a condemnation of the world we have made, and startling proof of the impoverishment of values that has left many young hearts so little incentive to great things. Surely never in the long tale of human anxiety has life seemed so unpromising to so many, and the temptation to "live up" the fleeting minute as though it were your last, seemed so irresistible—and so reasonable.

"What I would like to recommend for the few remaining years, months, or weeks that are left to us," says one to whom many of the young set listen attentively, "is to pass the time away enjoyably. . . . You may even find yourself sinning with greater zest—enjoying it, what I mean." Says a young poet and critic maturing in the post-war years: "It seems to me a lot of marriages now go on the rocks straight because of a feeling that there is no time to live with a failure. One has to make something of one's life—there's probably not much time . . ." It is curious, runs another sardonic aphorism in typically modern idiom, that "the nearer one draws to the grave the more time one has to waste. Nothing has the grave importance it once had".

The "sick" humour that our younger generation loves is full of the frustrations of mortality and the urgent four-minute menace of universal dissolution, though one is never sure that the probabilities are taken seriously or at all vividly imagined. A careful evasion of the truth mingles with the apparent acceptance of impending tragedy. S. Barton Babbage, writing on modern embarrassment about death, remarks a radical change in social behaviour-patterns in this respect. "In the nineteenth century, the processes of birth and reproduction were never mentioned in polite society, but the processes of death were an accepted subject of conversation. Today the processes of death are never mentioned in polite society, but the processes of birth and reproduction are almost a matter of daily discussion. Our grandparents, in their embarrassment and self-consciousness over the facts of birth, said that babies were found under gooseberry bushes; and we, in our embarrassment and self-consciousness over the facts of death, speak of 'passing on' "—or "if anything happens" or "sleeping" or "gone" or "no longer with us" or "had his" or a dozen equivalent euphemistic evasions. "These metaphors solace me not," was Charles Lamb's apt comment, "nor sweeten the unpalatable draught of mortality."

By way of illustration, Babbage contrasts the place of the death-bed scene in Victorian literature and its complete absence from the modern novel, and concludes, "without any certainty in the life to come, man finds the facts of natural death and physical decomposition too horrible to contemplate, let alone discuss or describe".

II

That absence of certainty about immortality is beyond doubt the heart of the matter. "In the younger poets," says one of their number, "the urgent problem is the imminence of death, the need of some significance that can be attached to dying in a world where there is no common belief in immortality." And a twentieth-century philosopher by no means prone to immature or emotional judgements has remarked that apart from religion with its undying optimism, "human life is a flash of occasional enjoyment, lighting up a mass of pain and misery, a bagatelle of transient experience".

The phrase "bagatelle of transient experience" enshrines the problem as age sees it, rather than youth. "Death finally runs the robustest of us down." Fear of death is not the sharpest anxiety born of our mortality: the deeper fear is that of life made meaningless and valueless by ultimate extinction, the deep dread lest mere oblivion shall crown the toil and faith and sacrifice of successive generations.

For what is at stake in the question of immortality is not man's comforting, but the validity of all his faith in righteousness, the significance of his decisions, the vindication of morality as native to the universe, the assurance of eternal justice and divine compassion, the underwriting of all man's high endeavour and spiritual travail as eternally worth while. The hope of everlasting life is not by any means the opiate of weak minds and cowardly spirits: it is the spur to heroism, it immensely increases the responsibility of decision, it feeds courage to face agony, persecution, and death with fortitude and uncomplaining faith. If death ended all, then life would be devalued, and man in the end prove only self-deluded dust.

This mortal fear of final insignificance underlies the wistful, universal, very human longing to prolong existence, if only by proxy, to achieve some permanence, to defy the passing years and assert man's everlasting value. For at times the sense of human transitoriness grows painfully keen. Earth's crammed with history, and we walk perpetually on the graves of our fathers: man is but a lodger in a great house that has seen generations of tenants.

In a great cathedral, whose styles and stones span centuries, we become doubly aware of our limited lease of time. Beside some ancient landmark still perpetuating long past events, poring over some hoary manuscript recording life of other times, handling some flint tool, studying some primitive decoration, revisiting the scenes of lives and battles that changed history, we can sometimes *feel* the passing of the ages, hear the rustle of time's turning leaves, and almost sense the resistless movement of life that hastens us forward through time as ruthlessly as the spinning world hurls us through the endless space.

This feeling of time's pressure can occasionally be undermining: "Let us eat, drink, be merry—for tomorrow we die." It can be humbling: "Dust thou art, and unto dust . . ." But it can also be ennobling: "Let us . . . so bear ourselves that, if the British Empire and its Commonwealth last for a thousand years, men will still say, 'This was their finest hour'." The commonest reaction, however, is to pit against life's transitoriness a demand for permanence and a stubborn hope. Heroically, or it may be pitiably, we cry out in the gathering darkness for something that shall live.

That longing may find expression in desire of fame, probably the purest of all pagan ambitions; to write, or build, or carve, or paint, or compose, what time shall not destroy. To win lasting . renown in battle, or (in these later years) in social achievement; to discover or invent that which will give our name to a new process, perhaps even inaugurate a new epoch; or just to live in the memory of those we love—all are ways of projecting our short life onwards past its limit. Perhaps the most human of all protests against the brevity of life is the ancient Hebrew desire to found a great family and see the third and fourth generation.

For our precarious impermanence makes us feel weak, and vulnerable, frustrated, and afraid.

> Give us faces of stone
> To set against the drift,

To set against the swift, strong, headlong
Currents swollen to a torrent
That is sweeping our world away . . .

Give us wills of steel . . .

Give us hearts of flame
To burn against the cold
To burn against the old, the mortal chill
The quenching thrill
Of the fast-flooding tide . . .

For we are little, and poor, and feeble: and we die!

III

The Christian reacts otherwise. He seeks permanence not in himself but in God. As the limpet's immovability lies not in its own power of suction but in the unyielding cliff-face to which it clings, so

Who trusts in God's unchanging love
Builds on the Rock that naught can move.

Not our will of steel, therefore, but God's will of inflexible love, says John, "abides", and confers permanence on those who do it. In the service of God's purpose from generation to generation there is a continuity which itself enshrines a measure of survival; it gives lasting value to our fleeting individual contributions, and so conserves something of ourselves. But more than this: whatever God wills stands for ever—"When God desired to show more convincingly . . . the unchangeable character of His purpose He interposed with an oath, so that through two unchangeable things, in which it is impossible that God should prove false, we . . . might have strong encouragement." And John means that those whose lives are freely identified with that immutable will and inflexible purpose are thereby invested with something of its timelessness and made heirs of everlasting life.

Faith, too, "abides", in the sense that it is not lost but perfected in sight; hope abides, in the sense that it is fulfilled, and not discarded, in attainment; and love abides, an unbreakable personal relationship which nothing present or to come shall sever.

But these abide because they are qualities of life itself and it abides, changing but indestructible. Of this, the strong and sufficient evidence is an empty tomb within an Easter garden, a risen Lord walking with men along evening roads of sadness, and appearing in shut places with the gospel of an ever-open future, and the continuing fulfilment of His simple, glorious promise, "Lo, I am with you always, to the close of the age."

So through its fleeting days the human heart can lay up treasure which neither moth nor rust can corrupt nor thieves break through and steal; an inheritance incorruptible and undefiled, that does not fade away but is reserved for those who themselves are kept. Of course the world passeth away, but in the world to come is life everlasting.

Thus spiritual quality abides because life itself endures, and life endures because God, its Source and Home, is timeless. Out of its hunger for permanence and for hope, above the stampede of the passing years, faith breathes "Thou remainest . . . Thy years fail not . . . From everlasting to everlasting Thou art God."

There is something to be said after all for Dr. Moffatt's translation of the twenty-third Psalm—"*The Eternal* shepherds me . . .". For the only antidote to human transience is the divine permanence, and the only satisfying assurance that of the ancient prophet, frankly realistic but resoundingly firm—

> All flesh is grass,
> and all its beauty is like the flower of the field.

The grass withers, the flower fades,
   when the breath of the Lord blows upon it;
   surely the people is grass.
The grass withers, the flower fades;
   but the word of our God will stand for ever.

10

"THE OPENING OF THE PRISON":
RELIGION AS LIBERATION

I

DOUBTLESS, to say that "religion is the sum total of all those superstitions and taboos that throughout history have hindered the progress and fettered the liberty of mankind" is to confess at one stroke an extensive ignorance of history and a total ignorance of personal religion: yet there is enough truth in the observation to make it plausible.

For religion tends naturally to be conservative, in the exact sense of striving to conserve the standards and beliefs of the past and convey them to a new generation. But the new generation ought always to challenge. It is native to youth to wish to make its own discoveries, run its own risks, and invent its own mistakes. The conservative spirit of religion must ever, therefore, appear to youth as seeking to subject life to external authority, to cramp and imprison the questing spirit within strict intellectual dogmas and moral conventions. What age venerates as ancient and tried, youth almost inevitably rebels against as "the dead hand of the past".

Moreover, religion is bound to exclude some areas of experience and some experiments in thought and conduct, as morally wrong, religiously unholy, socially injurious, intellectually false. Only a generation slipshod in thinking and spineless in morality would really find fault with a Church that knows what it teaches and is loyal to what it knows. Freud and the unconscious notwithstanding, it remains true that the gate is narrow and the way

70

is hard that leads to life, and those are few who find it: and no less true because some choose to misrepresent consistency and discipline as religious intolerance indulging a puritan passion for repression.

Scepticism and libertinism must save their faces somehow, even in the twentieth century, and a counter-attack upon religious "narrowness" is the obvious, if unoriginal, way. Nor can it be denied that Christianity has tended at certain periods to be merely negative and narrow: the necessary exclusion of ignoble and defiling things has sometimes been presented as an end in itself, the sufficient definition of the good life, instead of merely the pre-condition of positive achievement and divine enjoyment.

The whole truth of this matter lies in Christ's simple phrase: the narrow way of watchful and exclusive loyalty to Christ's high standards and example does lead to life—to the highest personal freedom, the broadest interests, the fullest culture of mind and spirit, the deepest enjoyment of all life's good things. And this is demonstrated not only in the claims made by the Christian gospel, not only in the lives of great Christians, but in the very nature of the Christian religion.

II

Religion generally, and the Christian faith in particular, has always claimed the function of inspiration. Its followers "mount up with wings as eagles"; in a dozen different metaphors it proclaims deliverance. It professes to add another world to this—two other worlds if the world within and the world above be held distinct! Its characteristic figures are pilgrim-travellers seeking faraway places and celestial cities, enticed by glimpses of a distant glory. Its songs are trumpet calls to enterprise, or battle cries of victory, or bursts of praise for new mercy tasted or new truth discovered.

Intellectually, religion has usually been blamed not for being restrictive, but for being a little too free with the laws of nature and of thought, a little too fanciful as to the powers of faith and of the spiritual world, a little too venturesome in its claims concerning prayer and immortality! It is unbelief that rivets fetters upon men's minds. Emotionally, religious themes have kindled a radiance of great music, painting, sculpture, architecture, eloquence, poetry, and prose, that has illumined the potentialities of the human spirit and awakened glorious gifts in souls that—but for faith—would have remained obscure.

The great motif of Christianity is *freedom*—redemption at a price and for a purpose, the liberation of mankind. In the synagogue at Nazareth, Christ announced Himself as "the opener of prisons", and throughout Galilee He proclaimed the truth that makes men free. As the dominating figure of the Old Testament is Moses the Liberator, leading men out of Egyptian slavery into the freedom of the promised land, so the dominating figure of the New Testament is Christ the Son, who makes men "free indeed".

The sayings of Jesus are open windows through which the hearer is constantly beckoned to larger truth than appears on their surface. The miracles of Jesus are living illustrations of His purpose to usher men into fuller life than they now know. He bursts in upon the dark prisons of the blind with deliverance and light. He breaks down barriers of silence that shut men off from their fellows with His gift of speech and fellowship and laughter. He frees stumbling feet from shackles and maimed hands from their fetters, to walk and work in the wide world. He opens dim-shuttered minds to let in the daylight of reason and normality. He ends the painful self-imprisonment of the inarticulate, enabling the dumb to express what is in them. He shatters the tomb.

Everywhere Jesus brings exhilaration, breadth, deliverance, freedom, the impulse to adventuring. This is the claim of Christianity: that where the Spirit of the Lord is, there is liberty, a wind of God that carries the soul forward on an endless quest for whatsoever things are true, honest, just, pure, lovely, and of good report.

III

Such claims are amply borne out by the historic examples of Christian experience. When Christ took Peter from his little boat at the village jetty by the inland lake, from a life of getting, cleaning, counting, salting, and selling fish, and taught him eternal truths, set him upon the search for human souls, introduced to him the magnificent vision of the kingdom of God, and led him as far as the capital of the world to the centre of history's stage—it is scarcely possible to pretend that in all this Christ narrowed Peter's life, or limited his experience, or fettered his mind!

Did not Christ immeasurably expand the life of Saul of Tarsus, when He arrested his headlong career as protagonist of "the strictest sect" of mankind's most exclusive race, bound upon a repressive campaign, and filling his soul with a limitless longing, his dreams with a world-embracing vision, sent him forth as Christianity's first passionate universalist to found Churches through the length and breadth of the known world?

So many of the great figures of Christian story are men who broke through the horizons of their time and disturbed the settled patterns of their inherited situations to launch out on new seas of thought, new formulations of the faith, new methods of approach to men. One thinks of Athanasius and philosophy, of Augustine and the crumbling of the Roman order, of Savonarola protesting against social oppression, of Luther and Calvin challenging centuries of ecclesiastical privilege and established dogma, and of Wesley, Damien, Booth, Booker Washington, Elizabeth Fry, Kagawa and hosts of others who blazed new trails for Christian enterprise, inquiry, and compassion.

Nor is it coincidence that so many Christian heroes have been travellers and explorers, breakers of new ground—men of the mould of Xavier, Carey, Judson, Livingstone, Grenfell, Nansen, and in our day Mickelson and Van Stone in New Guinea, Frank Beck of Bolivia, the Ecuador Five and innumerable others— whose Christian devotion has found expression in restlessness and wide-ranging experiments in world-wide enterprise.

Of course at times, and on certain levels, the Church has temporarily failed to keep pace with its thrusting pioneers and with modern inquiry: so that sometimes she has seemed the enemy of new ideas, the most reluctant of leaders. But this is true of every large social group; the balance between conservation and experiment is hard to strike. Yet the questing spirit of inquiry is native to Christianity—that is why scientific progress and originality are more marked in Christian than in Buddhist or Muslim lands.

Wherever Christ comes, with the message that this is the Father's world, and men the Father's family, that the future is bright with hope and the Spirit ready to lead us into it, the effect is always to open up new possibilities of self-realization, of spiritual adventure and social improvement, making the young men see new visions and the old dream grander dreams. None who have followed the Master's way have found life less exciting, or less enriching. The very variety of Christian experience abundantly confirms the gospel's claim that Jesus sets men truly free.

IV

But the final justification of this contention rests upon the nature of religion itself, and especially upon those characteristic attitudes in which the essential spirit of religion is defined. Without faith, hope, and love, there is—at any rate—no Christianity: and each of these is intrinsically an enlarging of the soul and a broadening of its world. Each represents an outgoing of the human spirit, stretching forth from its narrow and selfish and material circle of natural existence upwards, forwards and outwards to a liberated life.

By faith the soul rebels against the limitation of its powers. Faith breaks down the prison-house of the material and temporal and gives birth to the soul in the realm of the spirit. It links up our littleness with God's greatness, our wavering courage with God's unending strength, our fearful hearts with His almighty love, our life's little day with God's eternity. By the simplest exercise of faith we are daring to surmount the limited life of earth and hold traffic with the infinite.

By hope the soul rebels against the limitation of its horizons, lifting the soul from the narrow valley that stretches from birth to death, to gaze across the beckoning sea of immortality. The Christian hope bursts in upon life's little affairs with the revelation of an eternal purpose, and unveils to our short sight an eternal prospect—a new world where change and decay are but processes of growth and victory remains with life.

By love the soul rebels against the limitation of its interests, linking the individual to the larger Christian fellowship, uniting life with life and setting a man's eyes in the ends of the earth.

> O doom beyond the saddest guess
> As the long years of God unroll,
> To make thy dreary selfishness
> The prison of a soul!

This is the gospel of liberation. By the faith He implants, by the hope He imparts, by the love He inspires, Christ opens the prison of worldly selfishness and sends the soul forth upon endless adventurings of the mind and spirit, endless discoveries of friendship and truth, endless errands of mercy and of ministry. To commit oneself to His standards, entrust oneself to His strength, dedicate oneself to His cause, and enjoy oneself in His company, is to discover with great surprise the freedom that never corrupts, the glorious liberty of the children of God.

II

"LIKE TREASURE HIDDEN": RELIGION AS DISCOVERY

I

"MEN are led to religious faith by many pathways," says Professor J. Arthur Thompson, "from the perplexities of the moral life, from appreciation of the facts of history, from an experience of reaching the limits of endeavour, of emotional expression, and of intellectual inquiry." One might well add, "from experience of reaching the limits of endurance". Dr. H. R. Mackintosh adds as a motive, the "craving after fuller and more adequate life". A deep-seated need to find shelter, retreat and refuge from the harshness of life have also led men to seek in religion the alternative to despair.

Because men come by different pathways they tend to see the religious life in widely different ways. The classical description of Christianity is as a way of rescue, of salvation, the recovery of a long lost innocence and bliss. Or as an insurance against the strains, the dangers and the deserts of life—against self-reproach and retribution here, and hell hereafter. The twentieth century has seen the life of faith as essentially an adjustment to reality: God is *there*, and it is sensible to take account of His presence; duty confronts you, and religion assists in fulfilling it; life can be hard and exacting, and faith offers resources of courage and compassion; man is a sinner and religion does something about it; death is ahead, and it is well to be prepared. Such might be a typical modern defence: the fear of the Lord is still, after all these centuries, the beginning of wisdom.

76

Yet near to the heart of Christianity lies a view of religion which emphasizes not what man needs and gets but what he comes upon, all unexpectedly, in the course of daily life. He may indeed seek God for the satisfaction of some felt inadequacy, but yet make entirely unforeseen discovery, learning things he never expected to know, and experiencing the divine in ways he never anticipated. The old evangelistic chorus enshrines an authentic New Testament insight—

> He is not a disappointment, Jesus is far more to me
> Than in all my glowing day-dreams I had fancied He could be!

For "the kingdom of heaven is like treasure hidden in a field, which a man found and covered up; then in his joy he goes and sells all that he has and buys that field. Again, the kingdom of heaven is like a merchant in search of fine pearls, who, on finding one pearl of great value, went and sold all that he had and bought it."

So, says Jesus, busy men may turn up with their plough in the fields of everyday life an inner kingdom of enduring values and immense spiritual enrichment; may come suddenly in the market-place of the world's affairs upon a prize of incalculable profit—whatever they may give up for it. And that treasure, that prize, is simply to live under God's rule a life superintended by the overruling will of God, inwardly stabilized by the steadying peace of God, enduringly sustained by the living energy of God, quietly satisfied by the recurring joy of God. To stumble upon that secret amid the confusions and tensions of the modern world is truly divine good fortune!

II

But Jesus adds that only those who take life His way find *themselves*. "Whoever loses his life"—his soul, his self—"for my sake will find it", though to find himself, a man must first deny himself.

In Augustine's *Confessions*, one man's experience of God is clinically analysed. The result has been summarized perceptively as "the discovery, in the depths of man's being, of the absence of God in sin; the need and capacity for God in disquiet of soul; the coming of God in salvation; the recognized presence of God in the life of grace." That reveals as much about Augustine as it does about God—but it is ever so. Finding God, I find the key to my own being, the explanation of my own incompleteness, the answer to my deepest self-questionings, the Other Self, so wholly great, so infinitely good, that over against Him I know myself in my limitations, my inadequacy, my need, without despair.

Said Jesus to an eager young man of great character, wealth, and charm, "If you would be perfect"—a complete man living a full life—"go, sell what you possess and give to the poor, and you will have treasure in heaven; and come, follow me." So, you will find your perfect self.

III

Disciples of Jesus also discover *rest*. To take the yoke of Jesus and learn of Him is to find a rest which is more than cessation of strain or weariness, more even than that inward adjustment to outward pressures which modern people so often crave and so rarely find; it is refreshment, adequacy, freshness, an abundance of life that all unexpectedly, unsought, surprising, opens to the heart that learns Christ's secrets.

It is true that religion does not always achieve this serenity and richness. For some, it is more a discipline from without that stimulates and harnesses and prods the soul to higher-than-normal attempting and greater-than-normal achievement: even for these, faith provides perpetual inspiration for renewed effort. But for many others, religious life is constant advance in intuition of the truth, ever increasing sensibility to every impulse of the good, an unfailing overflow from a deep life within the soul where God is known and loved and enjoyed in simple thankfulness. To find that evergreen replenishment is to discover one of life's most precious, and most elusive, secrets.

IV

It is certain, too, that in coming upon Christ the individual finds *others*, inhabiting the same world and making claims, and contributions, that demand appreciation. A social psychologist might define religion—not adequately, but with partial truth—as the emergent self's adjustment to the social organism. "Religion is the discovery of people," said Coe, and if the aphorism is self-evidently incomplete it focuses memorably the Christian insistence that love of God and love of one's neighbour are inseparable attitudes.

For Jesus will not let us remain in ignorance of the existence of other souls, with their needs and claims and loneliness, their invitation to friendship, and their right to ours, their sharing with ourselves in the gracious purposes of God and the Father's equal love. To follow Christ is to be led forth from ourselves into a crowded world where much will be required of us and much, much more be given in return.

V

And Christian life is a perennial rediscovery of *Christ*. If the young convert cries with Philip "We have found Him", the older Christian with years of discipleship behind him will echo the prayer of the aged Paul, "That I may know Him." For Christ is the way and the prize, the Pioneer but also the Perfecter, of our faith; the Alpha and the Omega, beginning and end. He is "the Morning Star" heralding perpetually a new day and fresh opportunity and some surprising new discovery, for those who follow on to know the Lord.

There are implications, and provocations, in Christ's teaching that tease the most mature mind to further reflection and investigation; there are beauties and unsuspected depths in that peerless character which evoke ever greater admiration; there is a range in His impact upon the world, and a breadth of obligation in His challenge to His followers, that outstrips all attempts at definition and imitation. Nearer to the heart there are discoveries to be made of the patience and grace of Christ that our utmost prayer and faith can never exhaust. Only step by step, "from glory to glory", do we attain the divine likeness because only gradually do we learn the fullness of His stature. Only at the consummation of all things shall we "see Him as He is".

Until then, Christian experience is a series of glad surprises: as Schweitzer said, "To those who obey Him, whether they be wise or simple, He will reveal Himself, in the toils, the conflicts, the sufferings, which they shall pass through in His fellowship, till as an ineffable mystery they shall learn in their own experience who He is."

VI

The invitation Jesus brings to men is thus to come and make discovery, to find for themselves the treasure, and the pearl, and share the surprise of joy. "Come and see", "judge for yourselves", "seek, and ye shall find".

Look around you, for the living world is the garment of God, and grass and lilies and birds and sun and rain are revelations of eternity. Heaven lies near at hand in the glory of a golden day, and every living, breathing thing declares it is the Father's world. Or look behind you—search the scriptures: for God may be known in the things He has done, and the record of man's pilgrimage is the record also of God's long patience in seeking to communicate with men.

Look within you, for in the faithfulness of the diligent shepherd, the kindliness of the true father, the patience of the vine-dresser, the compassion of the good Samaritan, you may see something of what God is like, Who made them what they are. If you know how to give, how much more your Father! Or, look at Christ: for "he who has seen me has seen the Father"; and "henceforth you know Him, and have seen Him".

Discovery, then, may sometimes wait upon seeking—though not always so. When it does, the seeking must be sincere, thorough, persistent. The pure in heart, the single-minded, shall see God, Christ promises; and he who seeks shall find, especially if he carries his seeking to the point of knocking persistently at the seemingly shut door.

Such sincerity and thoroughness might involve painful self-examination. As one of the most famous and most perceptive of modern novelists has said, "Long years of wrongdoing build a kind of blank—or nearly blank—wall between yourself and God, and the task is to break it down. It isn't, of course, God who put up the wall; it is one's own actions and objections . . ." A psalmist said long ago, "If I regard iniquity in my heart the Lord will not hear me." Sometimes the great discovery waits upon eyes clarified by penitential tears.

Yet seeking, and self-examination, are in no sense the price we pay for finding. We cannot buy the treasure or the pearl: we cannot purchase God.

> Earth gets its price for what earth gives us:
> The beggar is taxed for a corner to die in,
> The priest hath his fee who comes and shrives us;
> We bargain for the graves we lie in;
> At the devil's booth all things are sold,
> Each ounce of dross costs its ounce of gold:
> For a cap and bells our lives we pay,
> Bubbles we earn with a whole soul's tasking:
> 'Tis heaven alone that is given away,
> 'Tis only God may be had for the asking!

12

FINDING A FAITH TO LIVE BY:
RELIGION AS INTERPRETATION

I

DR. C. E. M. JOAD, a popular philosopher in the strictest
sense of both words, had great fun with those eminent
businessmen who invited him to dinner with the express purpose
of revealing to him The Secret of Existence—as they had ex-
cogitated it in some treasured manuscript or treatise: and to his
entertaining description of these apocalyptic encounters Joad
gives the sardonic title, *After-Dinner Philosophy: The Universe
Unriddled.*

The gibe is deserved, for facile answers to imperfectly understood questions are characteristic of much religious propaganda,
and wide generalized claims to the effect that believing in Jesus
solves all the mysteries of existence on the spot only reduce
evangelism to ridicule.

Yet it remains true that unriddling the universe has a fascination
for all thoughtful minds; it is something of a necessity for all who
would face life intelligently: some clue to the meaning of
existence seems indispensable for serious and responsible
character.

Whether one concludes with Barrie that life is a wrestle with
the devil, or with Masefield that life's a headache in a noisy
street, or with Adam Lindsay Gordon that life is mostly froth
and bubble, or with Shakespeare's tale told by an idiot; whether
one returns to Plato's famous simile—"the life of man is like a
cave lit by a fire, and their perceptions like shadows thrown by

illusion, while outside lies reality lit by the sun", or to Paul's
"to me to live is Christ"—the axiom accepted determines the
whole argument of experience and lends colour to all one's
thoughts.

Unfortunately, science chooses to offer little help in this
connection. Lord Samuel, well qualified to complain, scolds
theoretical scientists for "taking refuge in symbolic mathematics
rather than answering the fundamental questions men are asking
about life and destiny . . ." Too often those who lecture mankind
on the marvels of modern discovery have—in the words of a
newspaper columnist—"routinized the combination of the
optimum rate of verbal delivery with the minimum content of
intellectual commitment."

Precisely! Yet what Professor Tillich calls the "anxiety of
meaning" remains to undermine assurance, and society's attempt
to anaesthetize the intellectual hunger by elaborating triviality
to the point of nausea, does not succeed.

Intelligent men must find a faith to live by, and if possible to
be inspired by. The Greeks, looking out upon a multitudinous
world, conceived within the chaos a harmonious cosmos, and
left us a legacy of beauty in which the truth they saw lies for
ever enshrined. The Romans, looking out upon a world of rival
forces contending in confusion, conceived a universe turning in
one ordered pattern of balanced energies, and left us a legacy of
law and statecraft that records their vision. The Hebrews saw in
the teeming creation an army of marshalled units moving at the
will of their Creator, worshipped the God above the stars—"the
Lord of Hosts"—and left us such an estimate of personality as
we shall never let go. Modern man has yet to find his illuminating
vision, his cipher for the universe; until he does, he has little
legacy worth leaving to those who follow.

If a man addresses himself to this perennial problem of the
healthy mind, he had better be sure—without pretending to
know all the answers—that the faith he finds is adequate. It must
cover all the facts. It is easy to select from experience the features

which support a prejudice: the balanced mind will seek some explanation that includes beside material phenomena the strivings of the saints, the insights of the prophets, the heroism of reformers, the steadfastness of martyrs, the onward movement of the religious vision in every generation, and above all the life, the character, and the cross of Jesus Christ. As Pasternak says, "It is possible to be an atheist, it is possible not to know if God exists or why He should, and yet to believe that man does not live in a state of nature but in history, and that history as we know it began with Christ . . ." That takes some explaining.

A faith to live by must work out well. The fruit of pagan creeds has been gathered in our generation in blood and violence, corruption and tyranny, the gas chamber, the concentration camp, the sexual pervert, the hysterical revolt of the lustful, the violent, the undisciplined, against society. As a man thinketh, so is he: belief in the long run determines behaviour, and the faith a man lives by had better be one he can live well by.

And it should make life worth the living. Irreligious theories about life's origin and destiny so often instil despair. In much modern thought, the individual with all his hopes and fears, his idealism and faith, his affections and strivings, his outreach after beauty and his climb towards the stars, appears the sorry victim of a thousand pathetic illusions, by which alone his brief and bitter life is made a little bearable! He is the product of blind biological development, a counter pushed around by natural, cosmic, psychological forces, dwarfed by the vastness of the universe and destined to return at last to dust and forgetfulness—without dignity, without achievement, without value, and without hope.

So declare self-appointed prophets of the new age of "progress": and all too often contemptuous theories about man prepare the way for contemptuous attitudes towards him. But the human spirit rejects the cruel creed, demanding a faith that will lift a man's head, and his neighbour's—not make him hang it shamefully in a sullen despair, or put it in the gas-oven.

And a faith to live by must offer solid comfort. Sickness and anxiety, sorrow and failure, age and loneliness, remorse, fear, death, are real, and only sentimentalists ignore them. Even modern hearts can break. Even modern consciences become burdened, tormented, afraid. Confusion and frustration impose a fearful strain. In such experiences the mind needs light, the heart cries out for courage, the soul seeks fortitude, the spirit aches for peace. To despise, or pretend to despise, the need for spiritual assurance in the face of adversity, perplexity, mortality, is not clever, it is callous. It stifles sympathy, and dehumanizes man.

II

It is by such tests—adequacy, morality, dignity, comfort— that we may assess the faith of Christ, remembering that His was a faith He lived by, grandly, and died for without defeat. Jesus believed in goodness, in being good. He believed that kindness pays, that truth is power, that justice rules, that tenderness is strength. He knew the meek soul cannot be hurt, the humble cannot be humiliated; that hatred cannot conquer love, though it well may crucify it. He believed that the universe means intensely, and means good. That is why, in Jesus' eyes, a man is wiser in the end to lose the world and save his own soul's good.

Jesus believed in immortality, which alone makes possible such faith in goodness. But the after-life, for Jesus, is no mere compensation, sky-pie for the dispossessed—like the Chinese communists' slogan "Work hard for a few years, live happily for a thousand." Immortality is life's constant background, lending significance to the soul and making nonsense of man's worldliness. The finality of death makes folly of life, and Jesus would not accept it. He rose again.

Jesus believed in man, of all sorts, and on all levels, and believed with an intensity that demands the name of love. He knew what was in man, both of good and of bad, and He saw men

realistically—as character after character in the parables reveals.
Yet their value remained supreme over all else in the universe:
and the worst was still a son of the heavenly Father for whom
love and a welcome waited in the Father's house. In all Christ's
thought man remains incomparable, spiritual, redeemable,
fashioned for eternity.

And Jesus believed in God, and if modern men are to believe
in God at all, it must be in the God whom Jesus preached, the
highest conception of God mankind has known. But can we so
believe? Can we be sure?

III

In the last resort, only by laying hold of God and finding He
is there. Yet that initial act of faith is no blind, irrational, wishful
thinking. There are, so to speak, five fingers on the hand by
which man reaches after God, five factors in the human situation
that point towards *the* fact of God.

The mind requires Him. Nature reveals pattern, order, design,
imposed on living forces, and pattern reaches backward in a
chain of effect and cause to unimaginable beginnings; the orderliness of nature is essential to science as it is significant to religion.
But orderliness implies a planning mind; the patterned movement
of the world implies a cause: and mind and cause must at least
be big enough to "explain" all that came to be. What is the
alternative? Reason itself recoils before the notion of a mindless
universe, and science dies.

The conscience demands God. Justice and truth, right and
value, love and mercy exercise an authority that requires to be
explained; what is more, they require to be fulfilled, and that
demands—in the ultimate analysis—a world that is not morally
neutral or insane but the creation of a good and faithful God,
instinct with a purpose of intrinsic good that becomes the source
of moral law.

The heart needs God. Alone, man is a poor, feckless creature, helpless, disappointing, bewildered, mortal. But he knows it, and yearns for what is permanent, ideal, worshipful. Through all the centuries, and in every race, the human heart has refused to accept a soulless universe. Man reaches out for God, and finds Him, and is at rest.

The spirit realizes Him. Poets, prophets, psalmists and saints all testify that God is there, accessible and gracious; in life's holiest moments God comes "closer to us than breathing, nearer than hands or feet." Something deep in man "senses" the divine approach in worship, prayer, and duty: and though that inner witness may be ignored, denied, or ridiculed, the effect is to impoverish man and darken all his thoughts. If he cannot trust that voice within himself, he can trust nothing.

And the Christ declares God. In answer to man's need, God has made Himself known: in Jesus, the subjective longing within man meets the objective fact of divine revelation. In the words and deeds of Jesus, God is real—has come near.

Thus faith has five reasonable grounds for its experiment. Experiment leads to experience, experience to understanding, and to assurance. In such assurance, of course, is no encyclopaedia of the sciences, no catena of philosophy! Rather, Christ gives the clue to the riddle of existence:

> I give you the end of a golden string:
> Only wind it into a ball—
> It will lead you in at heaven's gate
> Set in Jerusalem's wall.

Christ sets us at the central vantage-point of life, as though we were placed "in the middle of the Piazza of St. Peter's in Rome, where the pillars, which from the edges seem confused and patternless, suddenly come into line, all pointing to the centre". And setting us there, He declares He is the truth.

The only question that remains is—Was Jesus right? Is He the world's supreme expert in unriddling the universe, or is He, too, dangerously misleading because pitiably misled? Faith is simply betting your life that Christ was right, and finding in experience how right He was.

> If this fail,
> The pillared firmament is rottenness,
> And earth's base built on stubble.

13

DOES PIETY PAY? : RELIGION AS ENRICHMENT

I

WHAT a startlingly honest book the Bible is! Almost at the centre of this central book of praises, thanksgivings, testimonies, and prayers, comes this Psalm 73—an anthem of doubt, a frank confession of unbelief and embittered cynicism. True, at the time of writing the psalmist has conquered his querulous mood and found a healthier reaction to the facts that trouble him, but that only emphasizes the candour which still confesses, and records, this unhappy experience for others to profit thereby.

The source of the trouble was the very modern question, Does religion pay? Is godliness any gain? Does life really reward the good and protect the upright, or is it all delusion? Are not the careless, the indifferent, the ruthless go-getters, just as well off in the end as the conscientious and careful? Indeed, does not the prosperity of wicked people *prove* there is no justice in life and no God in control?

The psalmist understands himself well enough to see that his doubt is rooted in envy. It would seem he was a poor man, business failing, cattle plagued, crops withering, living on fixed income in a day of inflation, savings melting away. But the wicked prosper: they "live on the fat of the land" until

> their bodies are sound and sleek.
> They are not in trouble as other men are;

> they are not stricken like other men.
> Their eyes swell out with fatness . . .

The godless get on, "they increase in riches", and their wicked, oppressive schemes never misfire! This is untrue: but to the envious, cynical mood of self-pity, it seems so.

Nor does the psalmist accept that beneath the prosperous appearance is a troubled heart,

> For they have no pangs . . .
>   always at ease,
>   their hearts overflow with follies

because they fear nothing. They wear their pride as a necklace, their domination over others as a rich robe of grandeur.

> They scoff and speak with malice; . . .
> They set their mouths against the heavens,
>   and their tongue struts through the earth.

They are popular, fawned upon in society—

> the people turn and praise them;
> and find no fault in them.

Such defiant pride cries aloud for punishment, yet even God is silent. The prosperous wicked say

> "How can God know?
> Is there knowledge in the Most High?"

And God does not smack them down.

On his part, the psalmist, poor fellow, has been pushed around unmercifully:

> For all the day long I have been stricken, and chastened every
>   morning.

To him life seems full of obligations and conflict and striving to keep clear of reproach, to remain "innocent" of wrongdoing. A sensitive conscience keeps him alert, and the restless challenge of duty is ever demanding more and more of him—whereas the ungodly seem to pursue an even way, untroubled by inner doubts, and unhampered by outward storms. The way of the transgressor does not appear to be at all hard, to the toiling, earnest spirit fearful of offending God!

What then is the point of piety? Why should the ungodly be allowed to get away with it? The whole moral government of the world seems called in question, the justice of God, and the inherent fitness of things. But to that mood of envious comparison with others no spiritual insight is given, and the self-pity deepened into cynicism:

> my soul was embittered,
> . . . I was pricked in heart

and faith almost died—

> . . . my feet had almost stumbled,
> my steps had well nigh slipped.

Dr. Theodore Robinson comments: "It was here that he had slipped on the brink of the cliff, and all but been dashed to spiritual ruin" and proceeds to paraphrase the psalmist's brooding thoughts, "If that is what wickedness achieves, then, after all I must have been wrong. All my struggles for purity and innocence have been a failure; goodness is no good. I have let myself suffer pain and persecution for a phantom and a baseless dream."

And to add to the spiritual darkness, the psalmist dared not, at the time, give voice to his doubts or share with others the insidious unbelief that undermined him. He was half ashamed of his mood, anyhow: but he was afraid also of being misunderstood, of giving occasion to sharp criticism, of "letting the side down":

If I had said, "I will speak thus,"
    I would have been untrue to the generation of thy children

while private meditation only increased despair—

        when I thought how to understand this,
        it seemed to me a wearisome task . . .

II

until I went into the sanctuary of God

At length the psalmist had sense to take his doubts about God to God Himself, who alone can answer them. And he was answered.

Wrestling with his envy in the presence of God he gained, in a blaze of revealing understanding, a far truer assessment of the things he envied. A more just perspective exposed his gross error of valuation:

        I went into the sanctuary of God;
          then I perceived their end.
        Truly thou dost set them in slippery places;
          thou dost make them fall to ruin.
        How they are destroyed in a moment,
          swept away utterly by terrors!
        They are like a dream when one awakes,
          on awaking you despise their phantoms.

To understand this as vindictive pleasure in the downfall of others is wholly to miss the point of the psalmist's self-rebuke

        When my soul was embittered,
          when I was pricked in heart,
        I was stupid and ignorant,
          I was like a beast toward thee

—a beast without moral understanding. Worship has brought a clearer insight into the real nature of the prosperity he had so envied, as temporary, insubstantial, fading, vulnerable to the moth of inflation, the rust of deflation, and the thieves of time and death. It all can disappear overnight, leaving the soul naked, bankrupt, empty. Or the possessor may disappear: "Then whose shall those things be . . .?" There is little indeed for the godly man to covet in so "slippery" security, so "phantom" riches!

It was no pietistic dreamer, consoling himself for failure, but Lord Rothschild himself who said: "It requires a great deal of boldness and a great deal of caution to make a great fortune; and when you have made it, it requires ten times as much cleverness to keep it." Admittedly, earthly wealth is the key to earthly welfare, and is not to be despised: but the perspective of the sanctuary reveals that it is not worth bartering away one's faith and embittering one's soul for, either.

III

With the truer assessment came a stronger assurance. The crops may fail, the cattle die, the value of money decline, but God will not forsake His own: guidance in difficult times, counsel in perplexity, companionship in anxiety, upholding in adversity, and final glory—all are guaranteed:

> thou dost hold my right hand.
> Thou dost guide me with thy counsel,
> and afterward thou wilt receive me to glory . . .
>
> My flesh and my heart may fail,
> but God is the strength of my heart . . .
>
> I have made the Lord God my refuge . . .

Therein is promised a peace deeper than the most prosperous ungodly can know, a security greater than success can confer.

To know that however the winds blow, or the rains descend, or the floods rise and beat against your dwelling, the house of your life will stand when the storm is past, because it is founded on the rock of God's unfailing faithfulness, is to possess a serenity in which all envy dies.

IV

And with truer assessment and stronger assurance came deeper appreciation of the immense riches already within the psalmist's grasp.

> I am continually with thee;
> thou dost hold my right hand . . .

> Whom have I in heaven but thee?
> And there is nothing upon earth that I desire besides thee.

> God is the strength of my heart and my portion
> for ever.

> For me it is good to be near God.

Here is prosperity—here is treasure indeed. The gain of godliness is in having God: the profit of piety is—just piety. To glorify God *is* to enjoy Him for ever. "What has the worldling, when I have Thee!"

Religion offers no insurance against evil, no promise of prosperity, or even of outward peace. But it does offer an enrichment infinitely and enduringly precious. "All things are yours," says Paul, and Professor Tillich has commented, "The whole world is yours . . . the whole life, present and future, not parts of it. These important words speak of scientific knowledge and its passion, artistic beauty and its excitement, politics and their use of power, eating and drinking and their joy, sexual love and its ecstasy, family life with its warmth and friendship with its intimacy, justice with its clarity, nature with its might and restfulness, the man-made world above nature, the technical world and its fascination, philosophy with its humility—daring only to call itself love of wisdom—and its profundity—daring to ask ultimate questions. In all of these things is wisdom of this world and power of this world, and all these things are ours . . .''

If the claim seems too sweeping, hear the New Testament: "He has filled the hungry with good things. . . . Has not God chosen those who are poor in the world to be rich in faith . . .? as having nothing, and yet possessing everything. . . . My God will supply every need of yours according to His riches in glory in Christ Jesus. . . . We have this treasure in earthen vessels . . . the unsearchable riches of Christ . . . the riches of His glorious inheritance in the saints. . . . His divine power has granted to us all things that pertain to life and godliness. . . . Will he not also give us all things with Him?"

"Peter began to say . . . 'Lo, we have left everything and followed you.' Jesus said, 'Truly, I say to you, there is no one who has left house or brothers or sisters or mother or father or children or lands, for my sake and for the gospel, who will not receive a hundredfold now in this time, houses and brothers and sisters and mothers and children and lands, with persecutions, and in the age to come eternal life.' "

Large promises! But true to the essential genius of religion, which is—emphatically—a means of endless enrichment for the inquiring mind, the hungry heart, the growing conscience, the questing spirit, the developing personality, the advancing life. Piety certainly pays, in its own native currency and with accumulating interest. "Surely there is a reward for the righteous . . . I am thy shield, and thy exceeding great reward."

"O Lord, by these things men live, and in all
these is the life of my spirit."   Isaiah 38:16

14

"BY THESE THINGS MEN LIVE" : RELIGION
AS ACCUMULATED EXPERIENCE

I

INSIGHT grows by accumulation as surely as by analysis:
there is a deep understanding which results only from seeing
things in many lights and under many circumstances. The
experience of many instances, over a number of years or in
innumerable lives, can sometimes teach a truth which no one
instance, however thoroughly investigated, would sufficiently
reveal. Experience teaches, not merely by the multiplication of
examples but by the slow education of judgement, the steady
illumination of long thought, which no facile cleverness can
counterfeit.

Herein surely lies the value of history. Michael Innes makes
one of his characters speak of "the iron chain of Necessity, the
endless running out of which into the abyss of Time constitutes
the meaningless thunder men dignify with the name of History":
but we have had "meaningless thunder" enough in our century
to teach us to listen with new respect to the wisdom of the past.
Certainly during the storm we learned to draw steadiness and
courage from our history; and remembering some in Jerusalem
long ago who mistook what they heard, we do well to ask
whether within the thunder there may not be angel voices, or
even perchance the Father's voice, saying something we need to
hear.

Even Gibbon's negative view of history as "indeed little
more than the register of the crimes, follies and misfortunes of

mankind" assumes that history teaches something! It is at least a profounder view than that which represents mankind dragging its frail nets of memory through the sea of experience and catching nothing worth bringing to the shores of modern life. In Bolingbroke's half-remembered quotation, "History is Philosophy teaching by examples"—an insight which a Christian might prefer to express in the form "History is God's patient explanation to man of eternal principles." It is bunk only to those who choose to ignore its lessons.

The biblical Book of Judges illustrates the simplest religious philosophy of history. All goes well with Israel so long as she worships the Lord; when she forsakes Him, enemy forces invade and plunder until another "Judge" arises to organize resistance in the Lord's name and "deliver" Israel. It seems amusingly naïve, and superficial—but in fact religion alone at this time gave cohesion, morale, and common purpose to the rival Israelitish clans. It was religion which welded a nation out of the sporadic movement of nomads and forged a great destiny in the heart of a small and insignificant people.

No doubt the historic significance of religion can be so emphasized that economic and political factors are ignored: there was more than the decay of Greek faith behind the passing of Greece, and more than the assault of Christianity upon Caesarism behind the fall of Rome; the logic of ideals plus morale achieving power only to be destroyed by power's corruption, is only part of the story of the rise and fall of great empires. Yet it is part of the truth gleaned by man's experience: moral and religious conceptions do help powerfully to determine the course of history.

Herbert Butterfield, Professor of Modern History at Cambridge, who patiently discusses the place of judgement and providence in the human story, and made the piquant remark: "Perhaps history is a thing that would stop happening if God held his breath", has also declared: "It is impossible to measure the vast difference that ordinary Christian piety has made to the

7

last two thousand years of European history; but we shall have some inkling of that difference if the world continues in its present drift towards paganism. Here is a fact which blots out and supersedes everything that can be said against the Churches in European history."

An eminent American historian, Professor Charles Beard, memorably summarized in proverbial form the spiritual lessons which he felt the past makes plain: "Whom the gods would destroy, they first make mad with power: the mills of God grind slowly, yet they grind exceeding small; the bee fertilizes the flower it robs; when it is dark enough you can see the stars." And a third authority, now unfortunately identifiable only as "a second to none historian of our day", has said that "man's future lies not in the hope of his becoming 'civilized' but in the saving power of his religion . . ."

Yet it is not in this or that religious interpretation of events that the supremely significant truth lies, but in the emergence of religion itself, universally, naturally, powerfully, persistently, from man's common experience of the kind of world in which he lives and the kind of problems with which he deals. Whether from a demand for explanation of things he cannot understand, or from reflection upon the order of the universe, or from consideration of the nature of moral obligation and experience, or from terror of death, or from the personification of social pressures, or from the objectification of personal ideals and fears, or from the experienced incompleteness of human personality, or from any other cause we care to isolate and name, it is entirely beyond question that historically man has been "a religious animal". It is the invariable fruit of his corporate experience that he should seek earnestly a god to worship and obey. To return to Professor Butterfield for a resounding summing-up: "I consider," says the Cambridge historian, "that a religious interpretation of the whole drama of human life is the only one that is tenable for a moment."

If sometimes man's religious quest has led him astray into

forms of faith tragically mingling the best and worst in human nature, yet it remains true that the quest is native to humanity, and the highest results are a true reflection of the experience of the race. In the classic phrase of the concentrated moral insights of the Hebrew "Wisdom" school, "Where there is no vision the people cast off restraint"—which we might abbreviate fairly into "No worship, no welfare." For the twentieth century has provided its own evidence that where there is no wholesome underlying faith, no steadying apprehension of truth, no moral sinew of high principle, no inspiring purpose dwarfing our individual selfishness, no foregleams of far-off ideal goals, there people perish, however technically skilled and politically competent and intellectually advanced they imagine themselves to be.

II

But the accumulation of experience may equally be said to constitute the value of individual maturity. "There is a history in all men's lives", or rather, as Emerson replies to Shakespeare, "There is properly no history, only biography." What is true of the race is true of individuals: matured judgement turns wistfully towards religion.

The lessons of life, no less than the fear of death, lie behind the natural piety of old age: where cynicism and bitterness darken the advancing years it is invariably because unusual hardship, ill-treatment, or tragedy has made the heart rebellious or death unnaturally welcome. Normally length of days brings greater humility, simpler faith, and deepening awareness of dependence on divine mercy and strength.

Three of the Bible's old men may illustrate the point. The aged Jacob, lame, half-blind, and weak, blessing his sons looks back over his long career and remembers—first God, and the dream of Bethel on the night he fled, a "twister", from his outraged father and angry brother; next Peniel, and his repentance and the night of wrestling with the "angel that redeemed me". For Jacob recognizes in the retrospect of a chequered life that "God appeared to me, blessed me, shepherded me, redeemed me." Next to faith he names, in these last hours of his life, his love for Rachel. And next to that, he discerns and emphasizes—by adjusting his blessing to the natures of his sons—the significance of personal character as the supreme factor in the development of life. Here is one man's accumulated experience: God, love, character—by these things, the dying Jacob says, men live.

At the other end of scripture is the aged Paul, writing to the younger Timothy from prison in the shadow of the end. He asks for certain things, which Dr. Boreham calls "the supremacies of life"—for Christian friendship: "Do your best to come to me soon"; a minimum of comfort in old age: "bring the cloak that I left with Carpus"; intellectual interest and solace: "also the books"; and especially, whatever else be lost or left behind, the scriptures: "and above all the parchments". The details here are debatable. But the assessment of what the great man counted precious is incontrovertible: the treasures of the heart, in Christian friends and colleagues; the treasures of the mind, in the commerce of Christian thought; the treasures of the spirit in the word of God. These, with all they imply of faith and hope and love, are certainly the things Paul lived by.

Midway between Jacob and Paul stands good king Hezekiah. Gravely ill, he had looked death in the face, and seen much that once seemed important dwindle in size. He recovered, but the experience left its mark. In a poem of thanksgiving he rehearses his fears, his great weakness, and his new resolves. He has realized, in the face of death, what it is that men live for.

In a somewhat obscure phrase Hezekiah affirms that life now has increased solemnity, a new sacredness: "I shall go softly—go in solemn procession—all my years because of the bitterness of my soul." Such a sense of the inherent dignity and value of life is an imperative ingredient of all great living. But Hezekiah continues: "What can I say? For He has spoken to me, and He Himself has done it." A wholly new and nearer experience of the hand of God in his own life-history has given fresh meaning to his inherited faith. To hear the divine voice clearly in your own soul, to stand and see God at work in your own life circumstances, is to begin to live. "Thy care has preserved my spirit," cries Job, of just such personal visitations of divine mercy. Those who miss altogether such individual acquaintance with the ways of God miss the most exciting experience human hearts can know.

Yet still Hezekiah has not finished:

> Lo, it was for my welfare
>   that I had great bitterness;
>   but Thou hast held back my life
>   from the pit of destruction,
>   for Thou hast cast all my sins
>   behind Thy back.

Sickness has sharpened his conscience, fear and weakness have searched his soul; but with the mercy of God in healing has come assurance of mercy in forgiveness, and with opened eyes and humbled heart the king gives thanks for the deepest experience his life has brought.

III

Jacob, Paul, Hezekiah seize upon the same centralities: God, and the personal experience of His action and pardon; faith, love, friendship, character. The insights of such individual lives, and of every life of their quality, confirm the general witness of the race's history: that when man truly understands himself and his experience, he finds that the power, the providence, and the pardon of God have been at work in countless ways within his life. By these things men live, and in all these is the life of the human spirit.

15

"IF GOD SO COMMANDS" : RELIGION AS MORAL INSPIRATION

I

THE QUESTION was whether Moses could persevere in his enormous task, demanding vision, discipline, power of organization, patience, faith, and prolonged determination. Jethro, his father-in-law, thought the answer lay in being convinced that God had so commanded him. To believe that, was to possess the secret of invincible moral endurance.

Jethro was right, of course. To know oneself divinely commissioned is at the same time to find oneself divinely enabled. God's command, and God's promise of grace to make obedience possible, are but two aspects of one fact—the divine purpose that uses men for its servants. From man's side, faith and faithfulness are two aspects of the necessary human response: to know the purpose and to serve it are really one experience. Godliness is simply faith made visible.

From an exclusively ethical point of view, this concept of "the enabling command" practically defines religion. And the ethical point of view is after all a crucial one. Jesus declared it the supreme test of genuine religion: "Beware of false prophets . . . You will know them by their fruits . . . Every sound tree bears good fruit. Not every one who says to me, 'Lord, Lord', shall enter the kingdom of heaven, but he who does the will of my Father who is in heaven." When the prophet John sent from prison asking, "Are you he who is to come?" Jesus sent back a reply in the form of an account of things happening: "Go and tell John what you have seen and heard: the blind receive their sight, the lame walk, lepers are cleansed, and the deaf hear, the dead are raised up, the poor have good news preached to them . . ." Always His test of religious profession is, What does it *do*, What is it good *for*?—and His severest condemnation is ever reserved for those who leave good undone.

Moreover, the ethical test of the value of religion is the one which accords most with the urgent problems of man and of society. On every hand we are warned that character matters, and matters supremely. Psychiatry has impressed upon us the dangers of personal disintegration when faith and moral standards go: and the need for new techniques of character-development. Sociologists warn that anti-social, ill-adjusted, perverted souls multiply in modern society. Welfare workers are appalled at the breakdown of family and religious training that creates their gravest problems. Educationists are convinced of the urgent need for moral guidance in a balanced education for living. And many are finding nearer home, as domestic loyalties decay and personal relationships become embroiled, the desperate need for stronger moral safeguards in a world of merely hedonist standards and purely selfish values.

Certainly character counts. More than any other factor it determines our reactions to adversity, to temptation, to sorrow, and in the face of death. In every useful and worth-while aim in life, it determines our success, and our influence over others. In the last resort it decides our destiny. It is the only possession which is really a man's own, the only form of riches immune from the acids of misfortune; the only treasure that cannot corrupt the owner, the only wealth man can take with him when he dies.

But with the growing appreciation that all our focal problems are ethical, has come the sharp realization that without religious foundations the ethical problem is well-nigh insoluble. "Clever men are common as blackberries," said an earlier Huxley; "the rare thing is to find a good one." The Assistant Principal of a

British Prison-Service Staff College stated the essential dilemma acutely. Listing the social and moral misfits he had in mind—"the victim of imagined persecution who had turned on his supposed tormentor; the young sadist who had tortured his playmate; the youth who, surprised in commission of a crime, had resorted to panic violence; the young man who had killed the girl who had jilted him; another who slew a prostitute because she laughed at his lack of virility; the quiet young anarchist, and the noisy youth fatally involved in a dance-hall affray; the patricide and the matricide, the apparently motiveless killer and the sex murderer"—this authority finds it "an interesting but depressing exercise to examine the widely held belief that 'psychological treatment' would solve all" and declares "the crux of the problem is that we know little about how to change human beings or touch them at the level where the spring of action lies."

The besetting moral incompetence of an agnostic and hedonist society could hardly be better described; and in a generation when the influence of religion is denigrated, denied and scorned, even the traditional ways of changing human beings and touching them where the spring of action lies are seriously compromised. Yet these remain the primary tasks of religious faith: the reclamation of the sinner is the glory of the Christian gospel.

II

For all that, the moral issue must not be narrowed, as too often it is narrowed, to the individual failure, the criminal, the "prodigal". Society as a whole, and every worth-while agency within it, whether of improvement, research, reform, healing, education, service, compassion, or reconciliation, need constant moral reinvigoration, the nourishment of idealism and faith that shall inspire new workers with a compelling sense of vocation, and sustain both institutions and individuals amid the contrary pressures that arise from ill-paid and under-valued work. The young need to be kindled; those facing hardship need resources of courage and peace; the old need an enriching and enheartening hope, and those who carry burdens of responsibility in critical days need vision and assurance. When the moral tides of our common life ebb, and are slack, society is left floundering on mud-flats where misguided effort and undirected energy only increase the dangers of submerging altogether.

Religion's contribution to society's moral inspiration may be evidenced by two authoritative statements, the first in terms that scarcely reflect a zealously Christian viewpoint: "We can affirm that the word 'God' refers at the very least to the highest elements in the world of human fellowships, of social traditions, and institutions, in which we are all enveloped. . . . It means the highest social values of my group, the idealized spirit of my nation, of my race, of the humanity that is yet to be. It is the most broadly human word that we possess; he who invokes God invokes all the heroes and prophets of every race and creed."

The second statement is in words used by Professor Herbert Butterfield: "Christian teaching contains certain elements which will produce a softening of manners; in the ancient Roman Empire it stressed the sanctity of human life, the importance of the family, the evils of sexual licence and divorce, the wickedness of suicide, and the gladiatorial contests, and the murder of infants. Christianity was standing for a higher estimation of personality based on the view of man as a spiritual creature. Furthermore, the organization of charity was carried by the Christian Church to the point at which we can regard it as an original contribution to the life of the time. In the fundamental place which it gave to love, in its emphasis on gentleness, humility, joy, and peace, the Christian faith was parting from the ethical ideas of the pagan world and promoting a different kind of personality, a different posture for human beings under the sun."

But if authoritative verdicts do not suffice, our generation has ample evidence of the moral dynamic of the Christian faith in abundant personal examples. Nansen in Europe, Dupeyrat in

New Guinea, Pire among the war's forgotten victims, Gus Borgeest "the barefoot ball of fire", Stumpf among the shack folk of Hong Kong, Berggrav and Niemoller defending freedom of conscience, Henry Holland giving sight to one hundred thousand patients in Pakistan, Huddleston and Luthuli in Africa, Frank Beck of Bolivia, the dauntless five of "operation Auca" of Ecuador, Salvationist Charles Pean on Devil's Island—these only begin the roll-call of thousands who through missionary societies, Inter-Church Aid, international agencies, or alone, have helped innumerable victims of disease, ignorance, flood, fire, earthquake, oppression and war in our century, carrying supplies, education, skill, and compassion to the ends of the earth, building schools, hospitals, refugee camps, dispensaries, leprosariums, in every corner of the globe.

Henri Grouès, the "Abbé Pierre", vigorously campaigning for France's homeless, for refugees, for society's unwanted, "so that there will be a few less people suffering, and God will be a little less misunderstood", illustrates one compelling motive that religion awakens "on the level where the springs of action lie". Toyohiko Kagawa, writing, organizing, evangelizing, "slumming", "fantastically generous", ardently pacifist, "a luminous quality about the frail little man with the golden tongue" illustrates another, as he impatiently demands, concerning the parable of the Good Samaritan, "What is there to discuss? Isn't this plain enough?"

And Schweitzer illustrates a third, deserting a provocative but brilliant academic career in Europe to devote his astounding gifts to "doctoring with science and kindness" in Equatorial Africa, "living out his golden sermon" amid the cries of nationalism, bitterness, and suffering: because he felt "a simple and immediate duty as a white man to atone, if only in an infinitesimal degree, for all the wrongs that white men have inflicted on the black", entirely unsurprised that "the effort to serve the love preached by Jesus may sweep a man into a new course of life".

Our generation will have less excuse than most if it fails to apprehend the moral and social imperatives within the gospel of Christ!

III

But for the sinner, the saint, and society at large, religion's enabling command is personified in Jesus. Immensely strong, yet exquisitely tender, immaculately pure yet quick in sympathy and charity, Jesus lived and died in selfless dedication to the will of God and the need of men, continually in collision with the sins of the world yet undismayed, unembittered, unprovoked, and to the end unbroken. The character of Jesus still evokes from countless hearts not merely admiration but worship: in Him lies the supreme moral inspiration of past and future.

With that superb, unparalleled ideal, wrought out in Caesar's empire and in constant expectation of a cross, Jesus offers also an unparalleled faith to undergird our weakness and stiffen our resolve. Character is reborn in the stirring of conscience by Christ's example and love; it is enriched in worship, in fellowship, and in prayer; it is established and toughened by reverence for divine law and assurance of divine support. Without such faith, the moral problem defeats many individuals, not to say society.

Jesus offers moreover an unparalleled and enduring motive power. Simply by being what He was, Jesus releases the natural impetus of hero-worship, admiration, and affection. By doing what He did and does for men's salvation, He kindles a new and powerful motive of adoring gratitude. Most wonderful of all, He walks beside us, Guide, Companion, and Friend. The battle is lonely no longer. The secret temptation is known to a compassionate Lord, and He charms the warring elements within the soul into a disciplined peace. He is the know-how, as surely as He is the know-what, of moral achievement.

A life founded upon faith, informed with truth, directed by goodwill, upheld by honour, preserved in purity, dedicated to service, nerved by obedience, nourished with prayer, graced with humility, irradiated with charity, fruitful of social impulses, cheered with abounding hopefulness, and motivated by sincere and passionate love for Christ, is the noblest life a man can know. And it is never impossible, as long as life still lasts. For crowning all His other gifts in this moral realm, Jesus offers the unparalleled invitation to *begin now*—as, and how, and where we are. For He changes people. He specializes in making saints of sinners: it is His trade.

16

HANDLING THE PAST : RELIGION AS ABSOLUTION

I

"LIFE has no future when the past confronts you!"
The clever phrase exactly expressed the mood, a little
bitter, a little penitent, a little cynical, more than a little despairing, of the stranger who wandered into the Church hall, "looking
for a parson". He was well under middle age, but he had
managed to acquire a past all right. Escaping from an unhelpful
home, which drink and decayed religion between them had
made miserable, he had entered a somewhat hasty and none too
happy marriage, only to escape from that in turn into the excitements and perils of air warfare. Here, money had been plentiful.
feminine flattery abundant, drink had flowed, and for the first
time he had tasted the delights and dangers of "freedom".

It could not last long: but bombing-runs over Berlin ended
the spree sooner than might have been expected. Fear—plain,
stark fear—shook him to his senses, and then, as he realized what
he was engaged in doing, nearly shook him out of them again.
Grounded for "nerves", he came home at last a sadder but not
much wiser man, shaken, self-pitying, and tormented. For he had
to face a wife, and child, and the future: and he had a past, and a
conscience.

It was easy for friends to say "forget it"—easy and stupid;
for the sheer effort to forget, to stifle remorse with new defiant
excess, nearly cost him his reason. It was infinitely harder to
confess himself beaten and to turn once more under the

compulsion of childhood training, to see if religion could help. Hard, too, to learn the unpalatable truths that must be learned, to climb back to self-respect, self-discipline, and self-confidence; to rebuild his marriage, remake his home, refashion his whole life on new foundations. He had tried: he doubted stubbornly if it could be done: so he complained—

"Life has no future when the past confronts you!"

II

And the past confronts us in so many ways. Its influence lingers in memories that fester in the secret places of the soul. Remembered shame, now hidden, still confuses the moral judgement, paralyses the will, spoils every attempt at new beginning, breeds bitter cynicism about others' fine ideals and selfless motives. In nothing is the judgement upon sin more clearly seen than in the soiled mind, the stained soul, the blunted conscience, of the sinner. He harms no one more deeply than he harms himself.

The power of the past wrong reaches forward to the present also in enslaving habits, once *freely* indulged in but now unbreakable. It is not only the obviously habit-forming evils that bind the soul—drugs, intoxicants, sexual vice, gambling: fetters less evident but no less strong destroy the libertine's freedom and mock his claim—the corrupted imagination, the impure or spiteful patterning of thought, now almost beyond control, the undisciplined speech that soils and blasphemes unconsciously, the morbid, over-developed appetite, the uncontrollable emotion, the pathetically weakened will. When punishment threatens, the claim to "diminished responsibility" is the pitiable confession that the past has robbed a man of manhood. We are today the outcome of all we have consented to: as a man sows within himself, so surely does he reap in the kind of man he is.

Equally intractable are the tangled situations that perpetuate wrong decisions, sinful deeds, in unhappy domestic relationships, in lost employment, broken trust, alienated children, impaired health. How very many such self-created problems lend poignancy to the widespread longing to go back, and live life over again!

Nor may we ignore the cost of wrong in wasted years, missed opportunities, misspent life, the unfulfilled promise of early days. The omissions of the past are as powerful in punishment as more positive consequences, and as certain. Once-open doors are finally shut, and things that might have been are gone for ever. And the past confronts us in the judgement of society, and of our inmost selves. The wrongs of yesterday are remembered against us, and society can be extremely cruel, and unforgiving. Nowadays, perhaps, the condemnation of our circle matters less, because the standards of morality are lowered, and we move to where we are not known. But we cannot run away for ever, nor leave behind our memories. The inner voice remains, far more powerfully than we moderns admit, to accuse, remind, and humble us. So long as we have secrets to guard, we have not escaped the past.

All this could, of course, be stated in the longer, high-falutin' words that moderns love. The grip of the past is exercised through various subconscious ailments, compulsions, and inhibitions; in moral frustration; in "habitual negative self-attitudes" and personal unfulfilment; in the sting of the repressed good; in social maladjustment and over-susceptibility to social criticism; in the guilt-complex that feeds the death-wish. . . . Just so: what matters is not the name we give it but what we do about it. Phrase the matter how we choose, the evil we have done confronts us, like the elder brother in the parable, voicing the objection of our past to every fresh beginning. We have to handle it.

III

Modern thought holds, in the main, that nothing can be done about it. A physiologist has said that God and your friends may forgive you anything, your nerves forgive nothing and forget less! The psychologist might retort that whether the nerves do or not, the subconscious mind—into which sinks everything we do or think or suffer, to be stored up for good or ill in future days—certainly forgets nothing. The psychiatrist agrees, and adds, with Freud, that whereas most lingering ills of the soul yield to the treatment of being dragged out into the full daylight of consciousness, where the hidden secrets are guilty secrets, only religion helps. Even the poet joins the unhappy chorus—

> The Moving Finger writes; and, having writ,
> Moves on: nor all thy Piety nor Wit
>   Shall lure it back to cancel half a Line,
> Nor all thy Tears wash out a Word of it.

But what says the gospel?

It may seem odd that so many of the Bible's heroes are people with a past to live down, a life to rebuild from shame and failure: Jacob, Moses, David, Peter, Mary and Paul are but outstanding examples. Writing to Christians at Corinth, Paul lists offenders against God and society—the unrighteous, immoral, idolaters, adulterers, homosexuals, thieves, the greedy, the drunkards, revilers, robbers—and roundly adds: "And such were some of you. But you were washed, you were sanctified, you were justified in the name of the Lord Jesus Christ and in the Spirit of our God." Such emphasis is due, not simply to the sheer honesty of the Bible, but to something deep and characteristic and permanent about men's relationship with God. God has to deal with sinful men: there are no others.

So the great words of scripture are frequently words of hope to the penitent and mercy to the prodigal:

> Come now, let us reason together, says the Lord:
> though your sins are like scarlet,
>   they shall be as white as snow;
> though they are red like crimson,
>   they shall become like wool.

> Seek the Lord while He may be found,
>   call upon Him while He is near;
> let the wicked forsake his way,
>   and the unrighteous man his thoughts;
> let him return to the Lord, that He may have
>   mercy on him,
>   and to our God, for He will abundantly pardon.
>
> The Lord is merciful and gracious,
>   slow to anger and abounding in steadfast love.
> He will not always chide,
> nor will He keep His anger for ever.
> He does not deal with us according to our sins,
>   nor requite us according to our iniquities.
> For as the heavens are high above the earth,
>   so great is His steadfast love toward those who
>   fear Him;
> as far as the east is from the west,
>   so far does He remove our transgressions
>   from us.

And from the New Testament:

> My son, your sins are forgiven.
>
> I tell you, her sins, which are many, are forgiven. . . .
>
> Neither do I condemn you; go, and do not sin again.
>
> Thus it is written, that the Christ should suffer and on
> the third day rise from the dead, and that repentance
> and forgiveness of sins should be preached in His
> name to all nations.

Jesus gloried in the nickname Friend of sinners, declaring it
His life's work to seek and to save those who are lost, claiming
divine authority to erase the past with pardon. He is the Mender

8

of broken lives, Physician of souls, Redeemer of the race, Saviour of the world. His very presence in the history of mankind is God's own assurance that no man need despair.

IV

And Jesus *can* deal with the problems that the past bequeaths. For the stained soul, the blunted conscience, the debased desire, the unclean subconscious, He offers regeneration—a new nature, born again and born from above; with wholly renewed judgements, desires, outlook, tastes, and aim. "If any man be in Christ, he is a new creature."

For the weakened will, beset with habits and emotions too strong to break, He offers double cure: the expulsive power of a new affection, as awakened love for Him drives out all alien, contradictory loves; and the invasive power of His holy Spirit, as divine assistance pours into the bankrupt soul to restore its moral energies.

For the tangled consequences of past wrong, Jesus offers guidance and resource. Sometimes, indeed, the tangles are already resolved when once the heart is right with God. Sometimes they remain, but in wholly new light: the bitterness is taken from them, the resentments healed, the problems left are seen as spiritual discipline in which character itself is strengthened and refined. Over all—for the penitent soul—is the providence of God, bringing good out of evil and joy out of pain. It is truly astonishing how many times intractable difficulties melt away when once the will is set on doing what is *right*.

In place of lost opportunities and wasted years, there often is given an abundance of zeal and overflowing joy that crowds into remaining experience so much of Christian service and blessing that the "years which the locust hath eaten" seem restored. The condemnation of others is silenced—or answered— by a life transformed. Behind all lies the immediate, unshakeable awareness of God's pardon—of being absolved, here, now, at once, by a Tribunal higher than society and more authoritative than conscience, because Jesus died for the sins of the world.

Said Jesus: "The Son of Man . . . came not to be served but to serve, and to give His life as a ransom for many." He spoke of "My blood of the covenant, which is poured out for many for the forgiveness of sins." In the hour of His death He offered— for all humanity—the prayer that sufficiently explains the whole meaning of His cross: "Father, forgive them; for they know not what they do."

That is really all we need to know, to handle the past. The terms are simple, and the way is plain. It needs only that a man truly desire to start again—desire it enough to turn away in heart and mind from the sins he has loved, admitting his need, confessing his fault to himself and to God, to a friend if that will help, to the wronged individual if that will undo any harm, heal any hurt. And with the turning away from wrong, the heart will turn to God, without evasion or excuse, submissive and receptive, to accept the divine mercy and rest gratefully on God's pardon.

This is the gospel. "Repent and believe: if we confess our sins He is faithful and just to forgive us our sins, and to cleanse us from all unrighteousness. . . . Thy faith hath saved thee, go in peace . . ." That is Christ's method of handling the past. My Air Force friend is finding that it works.

17

SURPRISES UNLIMITED : RELIGION AS DIVINE INTERVENTION

I

OF ALL the Bible's teeming characters, no one (our Lord excepted) is better known than Peter. We smile indulgently at his impetuous blundering, we admire his vigorous forthrightness, we sympathize with his weakness, his fears and denial, we share his remorseful tears. And we all echo his dogged and undefeated "Lord, you know that I love you."

But if the humanity and frailties of "the Big Fisherman" endear him to us, his substantial achievements no less move our admiration. Foremost among the leaders of the apostolic Church (though not its formal head), target for the opposition of Sanhedrin and king, energetic in evangelistic journeying, to him fell, as Jesus promised, the opening of the kingdom of heaven to Jews at Pentecost and to Gentiles at Caesarea. We owe to him also a warm-hearted and heart-warming epistle, and his memories of Jesus add immeasurable interest and importance to the Gospel of Mark. Peter's later leadership in Rome, and final martyrdom, crowned a career fascinating in its variety, its winsomeness, its wide influence, its permanent contribution to the cause of Christ. If John is the disciple whom Jesus loved, Peter is certainly the disciple who loved Jesus.

Yet the outstanding feature of Peter's experience lies in neither his frailties nor his achievements, but in the astonishing series of wholly unlooked-for events that shaped his life. Peter is the man whom God surprised. For him were literally fulfilled on a dozen

116

occasions words spoken in another connection: "The master of that servant will come on a day when he does not expect him and at an hour he does not know."

II

So Peter's story began, in *an unprepared encounter*. Andrew, the gentler brother, had gone to hear John preach, but all that we know of Peter's temperament and language suggests he would have little patience with religious revivalism. In the morning Andrew returned with incredible news, "We have found the Christ." What argument and persuasion followed we can only conjecture, but at last Peter consents to see for himself—and the great adventure begins. Unsought, unprepared for, brought right to his life's door by a brother's persistence, Jesus confronts His man.

Jesus "looked at Peter" with that searching yet kindly gaze Peter was so often to remember and record, and said to him: "So you are Simon, the son of John? You shall be called Cephas"—a rock. Anything less rock-like than Peter's volatile, tempestuous nature can scarcely be conceived: but the meaning is plain. Jesus takes the initiative—*an uninvited approach*—and offers to change Peter's whole personality, establish his character, and build his life steadfast and strong. The *unexpected promise* comes unsought, but it opens a world of new possibilities to Peter's astonished eyes.

At Peter's Capernaum home, preparations to entertain Jesus at the close of morning worship were hindered by the illness of Peter's wife's mother, and on His arrival they explain the situation, without—so far as the record reveals—making any request for help or expecting a miracle. But "He took her by the hand and lifted her up, and the fever left her; and she served them"—an *unsolicited favour* never to be forgotten in that family circle.

III

An *unlooked-for success* next marks a stage in Peter's discipleship, for it issued in a totally *unforeseen call* and commission. After preaching from Peter's boat, Jesus suggested that Peter should thrust out from the shore and let down the nets. Peter mildly protests, "Master, we toiled all night and took nothing! But, at your word . . ." and the resulting "great shoal of fish" had a curious effect upon the fisherman. "When Simon Peter saw it, he fell down at Jesus' knees, saying 'Depart from me, for I am a sinful man, O Lord.' And Jesus said, 'Do not be *afraid* . . .' "

Clearly the incident had searched Peter's heart and brought home in some way his personal weakness and failure. He suddenly feels entirely unfit for the friendship of Jesus. Did he remember the earlier promise of remaking? Had there been countless secret attempts at self-reformation, all ending in failure —even as the night's fishing had done until Jesus took charge? Whatever the cause, Christ's decisive reply "Do not be afraid, henceforth you will be catching men" marks the end of Peter's hesitations. "They left everything and followed Him."

Months of exciting, absorbing instruction and activity brought the disciple-band to Caesarea Philippi and the crucial inquiry: "Who do you say that I am?"—turning point alike for the disciples' faith and for Jesus' ministry. In forgivable haste and endearing eagerness, Peter made the daring reply, "You are the Christ." As the sequel shows, it was an *unconsidered confession*: but Jesus at once accepted it with a glowing benediction and a promise of *undreamt-of authority*—"You are Peter, and on this rock I will build my Church . . . I will give you the keys of the kingdom. . . ."

Increasing intimacy with Jesus marks the closing months of the public ministry, and Peter is one of the favoured three on the Mount of Transfiguration and in the garden of Gethsemane, though one constantly feels he is being hauled along by events and learning as he goes. Yet this does not save him from the awful humiliation of the denial, and the bitter days of despairing isolation until an Easter message from the risen Lord brings him back among the eleven. Ere the forty days are past, he has faced out his failure with Jesus, and is bidden once more to "follow". Little could he have expected, that tragic betrayal night, that he would be allowed to retrace his steps and begin again: an *unbelievable clemency* brought to his soul forgiveness and renewed opportunity, and made him henceforth irretrievably Christ's man.

IV

Followed Pentecost, and the *unlikely choice* that made the man who had shrunk from a servant girl's accusing inquiry the spear-head of the Church's attack on the city that crucified Jesus. Nor was the sermon an impetuous harangue, but a persuasive exposition of the story of Jesus in the light of scripture. Once again the privilege came unsought: there seems no reason why he and not another of the one hundred and twenty disciples should initiate the Church's work. The pattern of his life still holds, and God does with him the thing he could never have anticipated.

In the story of the escape from prison, the element of surprise is especially emphasized. Even while praying for Peter's release, the Church cannot believe that he is safe and free though he stands at their door—but insists that the maidservant who announced him is mad, or has seen "his angel". "But Peter continued knocking, and when they opened, they saw him and were amazed." Nor was Peter himself any more ready for free-dom: the angel found him fast asleep, and apparently a little slow to grasp the opportunity to escape. On all sides, it was an *unhoped-for deliverance*, a rebuke to unready faith.

And the pattern held to the end. We may not assume that the legend contains more than a minimum of history, but it is surely significant that the last story about Peter treasured in the Church tells of his attempted flight from Rome and persecution, of his meeting with Christ on the Appian Way, returning to be crucified again, and of Peter's immediate retracing of his steps, to face death with courage. The mingled fear and fortitude, the initial weakness and resultant strength, are wholly true to Peter's temperament: but those who knew him in the early Galilean days would doubtless confess that the resolute manner of his death displayed an *unprecedented endurance*, a firmness of purpose hardly to be expected unless indeed some extraordinary vision of Christ had come to his aid.

v

Such are the highlights of Peter's exciting career—
> an unprepared encounter
> an uninvited approach
> an unexpected promise
> an unsolicited favour
> an unlooked-for success
> an unforeseen call
> an unconsidered confession
> an undreamt-of authority
> an unbelievable clemency
> an unlikely choice
> an unhoped-for deliverance
> an unprecedented endurance

—a round dozen of divine surprises! Let us admit, by all means, that the point has been heavily laboured for emphasis; that there is more to the story of Peter's development than this. Even so, it is spiritually and theologically significant that the story can be told in this way, as a record of unexpected divine interventions, little sought, little prepared for, and at the time little understood. Far from seeking after God, if haply he might find Him, Peter is at point after point confronted by God, though all the signals seemed against Him and all the doors seemed shut.

The Bible has a word for this aspect of God's dealing with men, and the word occurs repeatedly in the letter of Peter because the experience occurred so often in Peter's career: it is the word "grace". It means a free, gracious, wholly undeserved favour; the loving initiative of God to make Himself known even to those who look not for Him, who do not deserve Him, or understand—but do not resist.

Peter speaks of "varied", and "multiplied" grace, because it had come to him in so many different ways. He speaks of it as an inheritance, since it reaches forward to us from a rich past in which God made Himself known to our fathers. He speaks of it as a gift withheld from the proud but showered freely upon the humble. And he names God "the God of all grace"—one of the loveliest of all the Bible's titles for God.

Peter urges that we stand fast in the true grace of God, not imagining we owe anything to our own exertions; and that we explore, expound, and testify to what we have received, as "good stewards of God's varied grace."

All this, because Peter knows that in such gracious divine intervention lies all man's hope of succour and salvation. Here is a whole philosophy in a word: a gauntlet of hope which Christianity flings down to challenge a great deal of present-day thinking, and present-day fear. For much modern thought is dominated by the mental picture of a universe caught and helpless within a network of natural laws, inevitable results, unconscious, mindless forces self-acting through society, an irresistible chain-reaction of cause and effect against which it is futile to struggle, or protest, or dream. All is predetermined, automatic, "written in the stars".

The world becomes a closed shop belonging to the scientist —or the economist—who show us what *must* happen. The soul becomes a closed circle, in which all the life of man is tabulated and labelled, explored and explained, to conform to unchangeable equations. History becomes a closed series of events and counter-events, inevitable action and irresistible reaction, in a vicious circle fixed, fatalistic, and fateful.

Against the whole pessimistic assumption of the closed series and the vicious circle, religion protests that the in-breaking, uncaused, freely-intervening grace of God, "that bringeth salvation", has appeared and still appears in human life. No man's fate is fixed, and no man's hope is lost, and the world is not doomed to destruction, while God is gracious and determined to save. For He is free—bound by none of our rules, least of all religious rules: and to many and many a soul the truth of religion has dawned in a sudden, astonished understanding, and the joy of religion has broken in the glad surprise of the unheralded, unlooked-for, undeserved, intervention of the ever-gracious God.

18

"THE SAME . . . FOR EVER" : RELIGION
AS INVINCIBLE TRUTH

OUR THEME can be stated in two ways, abstractly as a
general principle, or personally as a declaration about
Christ. The result is the same: in the last resort, when all arguments are exhausted, and varying attitudes defended, our
decisions or evasions justified to our own satisfaction, it is not
what we think that finally matters but what *is*; not opinion but
fact; not our judgement as to what is true, but the truth's
judgement upon us.

I

Paul states this generally in a broad, bold phrase: "We cannot
do anything against the truth, but only for the truth." The
apostle is thinking immediately of his recent tangled and unhappy
relationships with the Corinthian Church, and urging that who
was right, who wrong, is best now left to the future to show:
the truth will stand, will out, and those whose positions and
intentions were true need not be very concerned to find vindication. The truth can safely be left to defend itself.

But Paul holds this faith on much wider issues, too. The gospel
is the power of God, not a message about power but itself an
energy of God, a living and abiding "word that works", for
salvation or judgement, for life or for death, in all who hear.
The spokesman of the gospel may be in bonds, he says in a note
to Timothy, "wearing fetters like a criminal. But the word of
God is not fettered". It can be trusted of itself, without the

meretricious aids of human wisdom or hidden tricks of practised rhetoric, to "bring forth fruit".

This confidence in the inherent power, the ultimate invincibility, of truth Paul may have learned first from his Old Testament, where the conviction that God's truth "endureth to all generations" is repeatedly and variously affirmed: the truth is indestructible.

Or he may have learned it from his tutor Gamaliel, outstanding Jewish scholar of his day, who advised the Sanhedrin to "take care what you do" with the Christian apostles: "if this plan or this undertaking is of men, it will fail; but if it is of God, you will not be able to overthrow them. You might even be found opposing God!" The truth is undefeatable.

It may be Paul learned this conviction from his closest companion and colleague, the beloved Luke, for Luke makes it the refrain of his story of the Church's earliest years. After the first slight rift within Christian unity had been firmly dealt with, Luke comments: "The word of God increased, and the number of the disciples multiplied greatly." After Herod's violent oppressive action, boastful speech, and sudden death, Luke comments again: "But the word of God grew and multiplied." After the dangerous imitation of Christian miracles in Ephesus had been vigorously opposed and a public bonfire made of books of magic, spells and curses, Luke comments yet a third time: "So the word of the Lord grew and prevailed mightily." The truth is irrefutable.

But wherever else Paul found this certainty, he confronted it irresistibly outside Damascus. Inwardly disillusioned, outwardly violent, mentally unsure, stung by the arguments—and much more by the courage—of the persecuted Christians, "kicking against the goad", he pursued the believers with the greater fury because of his uncertainty, until Christ "arrested" him, forced him at last to capitulate. The truth had won, he could hold out no longer. Truth is, for the conscientious, inescapable, and will not be permanently denied.

Carlyle declared that "the first of all the gospels is this, that a lie cannot endure for ever". Victor Hugo explains why. Writing of one of the decisive battles of European history, Hugo says, "The shadow of a mighty right hand is cast over Waterloo; it is a day of destiny. On that day the perspective of the human race was changed . . . and *He to whom there is no reply* undertook the task." The truth is God's thought, God's utterance, God's action: to Him men can offer neither counter-argument, contradiction, nor denial. We can indeed do nothing against the truth: it partakes of the quiet, unostentatious, unchallengeable immutability of God.

II

But Paul's abstract and general principle is focused and personalized in Jesus: the invincibility of truth is declared a second time—and in terms of Christ. He is the truth, the same yesterday, and today, and for ever.

In one light, admittedly, that familiar aphorism seems the very quintessence of conservative religion. In another, it is manifestly the perfect slogan for people who find their feet on slippery paths amid new conditions facing new demands in an age of change. That was its original purpose.

Hebrew Christians in the later years of the first century faced the decline, and decay, if not the actual destruction, of old and sacred institutions. The ancient order was irretrievably changed: the sacred was no longer sacred, the old ways forgotten, the old forms and rituals of religion were passing. The holy city, the glorious Temple, sacred altar, priesthood, and sacrifice were all threatened or already destroyed. Dismay, frustration, and an agony of doubt struck Jewish hearts as Rome invested Jerusalem, and Christian Jews felt no less than others the horror and helplessness of watching things hallowed by centuries of faith, devotion, and piety ruthlessly overthrown by Imperial might. A whole world of the human spirit, that once appeared invulnerable and enduring, was passing away, and belief in God Himself was severely challenged.

To men so shaken was sent this steadying reminder that nothing vital to religion was imperilled. Christ had gathered up in Himself all the living truth in the ancient forms—He is the perfect Sacrifice who ends all sacrifices, the perfect Priest who supersedes all human priesthood, the final Law expressing perfectly the divine will, the Originator of a new covenant replacing the old, man's Representative in the eternal Temple which is heaven itself. If He abides, in whom all symbols find their substance, in whom all truths are perfectly conserved, then nothing is lost.

> The old order changeth, yielding place to new,
> And God fulfils Himself in many ways . . .

Traditional ways of worship may pass, older forms of organization give way to new, ritual, symbolism, and all the hallowed associations of piety may be transformed, but He is the same—indeed, it is He who "abolishes the first in order to establish the second". We have an altar, a Priest, a covenant, a sacrifice, a law and an eternal rest—in Him who fulfils and focuses all faith: and *He remains*, the same yesterday, and today, and for ever.

III

Or measure the watchword against the changes of thought, and teaching, and language, that troubled the Hebrew Christians in that day of reassessment and doubt. Some—we read—clung too long to the elementary principles of the faith, afraid to move forward to maturity, still needing to be taught when they should themselves be teachers. Others were speculating, daringly questioning established ideas and preaching new doctrines. Old, trusted teachers were passing away, tested leaders who had spoken the word of God clearly and with authority. In all this ferment of challenge and doubt, this fear for the old truths and fear of the new, to what could the mind cling but to Jesus, the same yesterday, and today, and for ever?

To Jesus, by whom He who "in many and various ways . . . spoke of old to our fathers by the prophets . . . in these last days . . . has spoken to us"; He is the Pioneer and Perfecter of our faith. He is the Leader of the long line of great believers who through faith conquered kingdoms, enforced justice, received promises, escaped the edge of the sword, won strength out of weakness. He is the Son, in whom the Father has spoken His great last word; the final revelation of God, in whom all truth rests and is subsumed. Ideas, terminology, interpretations change, fashions of thought and new generations of teachers rise and pass away, but He is the same—it is for Him, as God's living and unanswerable word to man, and not for any partial opinion about Him, that we contend. And *He remains.*

IV

Yet for the average Hebrew Christian, the ritual and intellectual changes of the time were less urgent problems than the fears of persecution, the shrinking heart, the weariness of spirit, the temptations to draw back, to abandon the struggle, to relinquish faith and hope in the face of spiritual adversity. There is in the letter to the Hebrews, therefore, a clear call to hold fast, not to let slip so great salvation, to consider how Jesus endured such hostility against Himself, so that they in turn may not grow weary or faint-hearted. They are urged to run the Christian race with perseverance, and to maintain the zeal of earlier days when they had "endured a hard struggle with sufferings, being publicly exposed to abuse and affliction . . ." and the plundering of their property.

For the unchanging, invincible Christ is the sufficient answer to every external pressure on the soul. He is the Pioneer of our salvation whose delight it is to bring many sons to glory, the

Pathfinder and File-leader of the pilgrim way, Himself made perfect through suffering and learning obedience through what He suffered. He is the Elder Brother of all who face adversity, not ashamed to call them brethren. He is the Apostle and High Priest of our confession, able to sympathize with our weakness, one who in every respect has been tempted as we are, yet without sinning, and so able to help those who are tempted.

And Jesus is all this unchangingly: though our courage ebbs and our feelings fluctuate and the cause wavers and comrades dwindle, yet *He remains*, able for all time to save those who draw near to God through Him, since He always lives to make intercession for them.

v

Irrespective, then, of our opinion or choice, the truth remains, indestructible, invincible, and ultimately inescapable; irrespective of our faith or unbelief, Christ remains, unchanging, unchallengeable, and in the end not to be evaded. In Gerard van Honthorst's painting of Christ before the High Priest, a single candle stands on the table between the Prisoner and His interrogator; its light falls gently on the face of Jesus, and upon the open page of scripture before the priest: but it falls with brilliance upon the face of Caiaphas—every line and wrinkle of that aged countenance, every gleam of those cold appraising eyes, is sharply defined. Whatever the interrogation revealed about Christ, it exposed the selfish motives, the ruthless, unprincipled expediency, the time-serving diplomacy of the worldly leader of Jewry—even as the later Roman trial exposed the cowardice and incompetence of Pilate. It is never Jesus who is on trial: never the truth which is being tested. Our every assessment of Christ, and of truth, merely exposes ourselves.

It is precisely this absoluteness of religious truth, the exclusiveness of Christian claims for Christ, the intolerance of the challenge to Christian faith and obedience as the *only* hope of human salvation, which offends the easy-going, relativist, compromising modern mind. We abhor dogmatism—except when it introduces its pronouncements with either "Science says . . ." or "Most people think . . ." But the preference for indecision, for noncommitment, for all cats grey and all paradoxes and contradictions "equally true", is intellectual and logical nonsense and moral evasion. Truth is absolutely true; right is eternally right, and no cultivated neutralism of ours can change it.

So, it is not in our power to decide if religion be true or false, only to decide our own reaction, and so determine our own destiny. It is not for us to sit in judgement upon Jesus, only to accept or reject Him, and so determine His judgement of us. The world passeth away, and we with it: but truth endures and Christ remains—and he who does the will of God abides for ever.

ACKNOWLEDGEMENTS

Grateful acknowledgement is made of passages quoted and opinions cited as follow:

Throughout, scripture quotations are from the Revised Standard Version of the Bible, copyrighted 1946 and 1952, used by permission;

IN SERMON 1—from an unsigned article in *The Modern Churchman*, Blackwell, Oxford; from F. W. Boreham: *The Luggage of Life*, Epworth Press, 3rd (Pocket) Edition, 1934, p. 204; from Fred Hoyle: *The Nature of the Universe*, Blackwell, 1950, p. 72; from F. W. Faber: "The Greatness of God";

IN SERMON 2—from W. Lippmann, as reported; from Aldous Huxley: *Ends and Means*, Chatto and Windus, 1937, pp. 124, 72;

IN SERMON 3—from M. Farrow: "Prayer from the Brink" (*Anthology of Religious Verse*, edited Norman Nicholson, Penguin Books 1942: copyright untraceable); from Jean Ingelow: "I am glad to think";

IN SERMON 4—from Matthew Arnold: "To Marguerite, Isolation"; from S. Rogers: "Human Life"; from Alice Meynell: "He Rose Again" (by permission of Burns and Oates, Ltd.);

IN SERMON 5—from Miss Helen Keller's contribution to a symposium, *This I Believe*, Hamish Hamilton; from Walt Whitman: "A noiseless patient spider";

IN SERMON 6—from Lord Samuel, speech to British House of Lords, November 4th 1953; from Bryan Wilson and Malcolm Bradbury, article entitled "Fleet Street and the Crime Wave" in *The Guardian* (Manchester, England);

IN SERMON 7—from reported interview with Henry Miller, in *The Guardian* (above); from Paul Tillich: *The New Being*, S.C.M. Press, 1956, p. 38f.; from Lewis Mumford, cited in J. Isaacs: *Assessment of Twentieth Century Literature*, Secker and Warburg, 1951; from Sir Julian Huxley: *The Humanist Frame*, Geo. Allen and Unwin, 1961, pp. 21, 14; from anonymous article, "The Art of Healing", London *Sunday Times*, September 28th 1953;

IN SERMON 8—from John Watson: *The Mind of the Master*; from Sir Julian Huxley: *The Humanist Frame* (above), p. 41; *Religion Without Revelation*, Parrish, London; Harper, New York, 1957, pp. 306, 9, 52, 72; from Gibbon: *Decline and Fall*, vol. 1, chap. 2; from Aldous Huxley: *Ends and Means* (above), pp. 274, 268; from Jung, cited in W. S. Urquhart: *Humanism and Christianity*, T. & T. Clark, 1945, pp. 29, 30; from D. S. Cairns: *Riddle of the World*, 1937, p. 33; from T. S. Eliot: essay in *Revelation* (edited J. Baillie, H. Martin), 1927, p. 5; from Hartshorne: *Beyond Humanism*, p. 2, and De Burgh: *Towards a Religious Philosophy*, p. 161, cited in Urquhart (above); from A. N. Whitehead: *Science and the Modern World*, Mentor Edition, New York, 1948, p. 91; from J. Maritain: *True Humanism*, Geoffrey Bles, 1938, p. 11; from N. Berdyaev: *Freedom and the Spirit*, Geoffrey Bles, 1935, p. 53; from W. S. Urquhart: *Humanism and Christianity* (above), p. 21; from F. R. Barry: *Relevance of Christianity*, Nisbet, 1931, p. 129; from Edward Shillito: "Jesus of the Scars", used by permission;

IN SERMON 9—from reported interview with Henry Miller (above); from A. Alvarez and D. Davie, in *Review*, Oxford, April/May 1962, p. 18f.; from S. Barton Babbage, in *Christianity Today*, vol. 2, no. 9 (February 3, 1958), p. 9; from George Every: "Designs for Culture", *Humanities*, vol. ii, no. 2, 1948, cited by Babbage; from A. N. Whitehead: *Science and the Modern World* (above), p. 171; from M. Farrow: "Prayer from the Brink" (see above);

IN SERMON 10—from J. G. Whittier: "The Answer";

IN SERMON 11—from A. Schweitzer: *Quest of the Historical Jesus*, A. and C. Black (3rd edition) 1954, p. 461; from Dame Rose Macaulay: *Letters to a Friend* 1950-52, edited by Constance Babington Smith, Collins, 1961, p. 39; from J. R. Lowell: "Vision of Sir Launfal", Prelude, part 1;

IN SERMON 12—from C. E. M. Joad: *Return to Philosophy*, Faber and Faber (edition of 1945), pp. 9, 10; from Boris Pasternak: *Dr Zhivago*, Collins/Harvill, 1958, p. 19; from William Blake: "The Golden String"; from John Milton: *Comus*;

IN SERMON 13—from T. H. Robinson in Oesterley: *The Psalms*, S.P.C.K., 1955, p. 343; from Paul Tillich: *The New Being* (above);

IN SERMON 14—from Michael Innes: *From London Far*, Penguin Books, 1962, p. 8; from H. Butterfield: *Christianity and History*, Geo. Bell and Sons, 1949, pp. 111, 131f., 132;

In Sermon 15—from Mr. Gordon Hawkins, assist. Principal, Prison Service Staff College, Wakefield, England, in *Criminal Law Review*, October 1960; from W. M. Horton: *Psychological Approach to Theology*, p. 199 (cited in Urquhart); from H. Butterfield: *Christianity in European History*, Collins, 1952, pp. 14-15;

In Sermon 16—from E. FitzGerald: *Rubaiyat of Omar Khayyam*, stanza 51;

In Sermon 18—from Victor Hugo: *Les Misérables*, Part II, Book, 1, chap. 13 *ad finem*.